Warning Shadows

German Film Classics

Series Editors

Gerd Gemünden, Dartmouth College
Johannes von Moltke, University of Michigan

Advising Editors

Anton Kaes, University of California-Berkeley
Eric Rentschler, Harvard University

Editorial Board

Also in the series:

WARNING SHADOWS

ANJEANA K. HANS

CAMDEN HOUSE

First published 2021 by Camden House

Camden House is an imprint of Boydell & Brewer Inc.
668 Mt. Hope Avenue, Rochester, NY 14620, USA
and of Boydell & Brewer Limited
PO Box 9, Woodbridge, Suffolk IP12 3DF, UK
www.boydellandbrewer.com

Cover image: The illusionist's skills with shadow play. Screenshot.

ISBN-13: 978-1-64014-091-2

Library of Congress Cataloging-in-Publication Data

CIP data is available from the Library of Congress.

This publication is printed on acid-free paper.
Printed in the United States of America.

Publication of this book was supported by a grant from the German Film Institute (GFI) of the University of Michigan Department of Germanic Languages & Literatures.

CONTENTS

ACKNOWLEDGMENTS

Like so many books, this one got its start at a conference, at a celebration, in fact, of the launch of the series in which this book appears. The first thank-yous go to Barbara Hales, Ervin Malakaj, and Valerie Weinstein, the dear colleagues who didn't just listen to me say how apt *Warning Shadows* is for the series, but rather told me to go suggest it to the editors right that minute, and to the series editors, Gerd Gemünden and Johannes von Moltke, who were so generous in the care with which they listened to my hasty pitch and the enthusiasm that they showed. Joel Westerdale, whom I already owed thanks from when I first wrote about *Warning Shadows*, earned more gratitude this time around when he not only talked through this fascinating and too often overlooked film with me again, but also encouraged me in my belief that this is a necessary book. The series editors and the anonymous reviewer gave me the kind of thoughtful feedback and gentle suggestions that allowed me to make the manuscript one that I'm truly proud of. And an enormous thank you to Philipp Stiasny, who not only checked in periodically with encouragement, but also is an unfailingly generous and seemingly endless source for the kinds of references, connections, and sidenotes that are so central to understanding *Warning Shadows*.

My fascination with *Warning Shadows* goes back to my work on my first book, *Gender and the Uncanny in Films of the Weimar Republic* (Wayne State UP, 2014). I started researching the background and the response to the movie at the Kinemathek in Berlin as early as 2008, and was generously supported by grants to do so, first by Tulane University and later by Wellesley College. The material that I found but didn't necessarily use at the time formed the basis of this book, where I set out to re-evaluate the film more broadly than I did in my first project.

Many thanks to everyone at Camden House, who has demonstrated at every turn professionalism, expertise, and grace; and especially to Jim Walker, whose unflagging enthusiasm, patience, and encouragement made this project possible, and whose careful reading and detailed feedback improved everything about this book.

Finally and always, my thanks to my family, especially my mother, who is certain I can dash off a book in my spare time with no problem, and my big sister, who will likely be buying this book to give as gifts for years to come. My grateful love and hugs to my kids, who insist that elementary-schoolers can surely read a book this slim and with this many pictures, and also that I can interrupt my work at any time in order to play Lego. And my everlasting gratitude to Nate, who keeps our life on track on the many occasions when there's a deadline looming or I'm buried in a project, and who makes everything—even a pandemic!—fun.

Warning Shadows

Introduction: A Little-Known Movie

It's fair to say that, when one thinks about the major films associated with Weimar Germany's thriving film industry, *Schatten* (released in English as *Warning Shadows*, 1923) is not among the titles that immediately come to mind. Enthusiasts of early cinema would more likely mention Robert Wiene's *Das Cabinet des Dr. Caligari* (*The Cabinet of Dr. Caligari*, 1920), today often viewed as the film that best exemplifies cinematic Expressionism with its stylized visuals and its focus on madness and uncertainty; or Murnau's *Nosferatu* (1922), the first and unauthorized movie of Bram Stoker's *Dracula* (1897), which led to a lawsuit for copyright infringement and the bankruptcy of producer Albin Grau's Prana-Film company; or Fritz Lang's monumental *Metropolis* (1927), which had a brief revival in 1984 with Giorgio Moroder's restoration setting it to music by Freddie Mercury, Pat Benatar, and others; or Josef von Sternberg's *Der blaue Engel* (*The Blue Angel*, 1930), not Marlene Dietrich's film debut, but nevertheless the performance that set her on the path to international stardom. Names like Ernst Lubitsch, who directed comedies and historical spectacles in Berlin before leaving Berlin for Hollywood and Mary Pickford in 1922, or G. W. Pabst, whose films starred many of Weimar Germany's best-known female actors including Greta Garbo, Brigitte Helm, and Asta Nielsen, are likely far more familiar to most than that of Artur Robison, the director of *Warning Shadows*, whose name, even at the time, was all too frequently misspelled in articles as "Arthur Robinson."

And yet, *Warning Shadows* is a movie that connects with so much of Weimar culture, that demonstrates and problematizes so many of the visual and generic characteristics associated with the cinema of the time, and that is, quite frankly, just odd enough to be truly interesting. The story begins simply enough: a traveling illusionist (Alexander Granach) gains entrance into a house where a wealthy couple is entertaining four men, all of whom admire the wife (Ruth Weyher) quite openly, and one of whom (Gustav von Wangenheim) sees his flirtation with her reciprocated. From here, the narrative becomes much less simple, comprising multiple layers of projection, illusion, and performance: seeing the dangerous path of the two would-be lovers, the illusionist stages a doubled performance, first projecting a Chinese shadow play about infidelity, then hypnotizing the spectators so that they take part in a "shadow play" of their own. In this (hallucinated?) episode, the husband (Fritz Kortner) witnesses his wife's infidelity, has her dragged into the room and bound to the table, and forces her assembled admirers to stab her to death. He then collapses in despair, and the other men, finding their courage only after participating in the woman's murder, throw him out of the window. But his dead body in the courtyard outside represents only the end of the hallucinatory shadow play: the assembled group wakes up from this strange episode unscathed and watches the remainder of the Chinese shadow play. The happy ending of that performance prefigures that of the film as a whole: husband and wife send the illusionist and the woman's admirers on their way and embrace as they look out at the morning scene of a market being set up in the courtyard outside. The rising sun suggests a literal and metaphorical new day for them.

In spite of the multiple layers, the narrative of *Warning Shadows* conforms to the Aristotelian unities: the action takes place only in a single "night of realization," as the movie was subtitled in some markets,[1] and in a single location. The cast is small, comprising, outside of the crowd we see setting up the market at the very end, just the couple, the illusionist, the four guests, a maid and two servants, and three musicians who only appear briefly. But that apparent simplicity is belied by the multiple stories-within-the-story, or perhaps more precisely the projections-within-the-projection: not only the Chinese shadow play, but also glimpses showing the husband's memories and fantasies and the hallucinatory episode. Even this is complicated: by repeated moments in which we see shadows, silhouettes, and reflections—on walls, on doors, on drapes, in mirrors. *Warning Shadows* becomes a sort of nesting doll of a movie, a projection that holds within it innumerable others. Indeed, one especially interesting aspect of the film is the way it reflects on itself and on the medium of film. James C. Franklin sees the many moments in which the film exposes to the spectator how shadows are misinterpreted as even more compelling than the central hallucination, in that they reveal how "Robison himself becomes an illusionist for *his* audience, showing us truths that are invisible to the characters themselves and intriguingly ambiguous to us."[2] In *Warning Shadows*, it is in many ways unclear where exactly the hallucination ends and "life" begins. We can ask what this blurring of boundaries says, not just about the movie itself, but also about cinema as a medium.

As a viewer of silent film and a scholar of gender, film, and Weimar culture, I find it perplexing to see how little-known *Warning Shadows* is. To start, it's a movie that is fun to watch: visually interesting, at times shocking, and with a convincing cast. Its obscurity isn't due simply to its being difficult to find: Kino Video released a DVD version in 2006, it was available in the US, at least for a while, on Netflix and Amazon Prime streaming, and French-German television channel ARTE screened and released a restored version in 2016. As one of the fairly small number of films from the Weimar era that is widely accessible in a high-quality restoration, *Warning Shadows* might be expected to have a stronger presence, whether as a part of film syllabi or as straightforward entertainment. It's interesting stylistically, as well: some of its characteristics exemplify what we associate with expressionism, and yet others run counter to the way we define that term. One reviewer at the time noted with approval that the filmmakers "eschewed today's all-too-tacky expressionism" and instead drew on "that most primary of cinematographic tools: light."[3] That review, suggesting that there existed different "types" of expressionism, is a reminder that even so apparently ubiquitous a term is not as clearly defined as we think. Sabine Hake has suggested that Expressionism designates not so much a specific style as a mode of functioning: expressionist film draws vision into question, emphasizing the illusory nature of appearance and destabilizing the notion of the subject itself.[4] To be sure, there is much in *Warning Shadows* that aligns with this. Vision is deceptive and contested, indelibly shaped by the jealousy that dominates the husband and the desire that motivates the woman and her admirers. Yet the ways in which *Warning Shadows* differs from the "trite" style of expressionism referenced by the reviewer, eschewing, for example, the stylized sets of a film like *Caligari*, emphasizes the fluidity of the term.

In terms of genre, too, *Warning Shadows* is no easy fit, and pushes us to question the way we try to categorize early film generically. In its foregrounding of the hallucinatory interior episode, it connects to the uncanny films we so often associate with Weimar expressionist cinema. But to call *Warning Shadows* a fantastic film, or a thriller, or even a tale of terror, as S. S. Prawer termed it and other expressionist films including *Caligari*,[5] doesn't quite ring true. Instead, we see elements that link it to multiple genres: its emphasis on the domestic, its claustrophobic setting, and its small cast aligns it with the *Kammerspiel*, the "chamber drama" that staged narratives bound up with and constrained by intimate ties and spaces. The depiction of the dangers of "base passions" and desires resonates with the *Aufklärungsfilme* (enlightenment or social hygiene films) that Richard Oswald pioneered. And its dramatization of psychological interiority, coupled with the emphasis on hypnosis and on unconscious desires, links it on one hand to films like *Caligari*, where the motif of hypnosis is bound up with power and control, and on the other to those like Pabst's *Geheimnisse einer Seele* (*Secrets of a Soul*,

Figure 1. The opening shot with the illusionist's hand.

1926), where film becomes a means of exploring the unconscious and hypnosis acts as therapeutic tool.

The ambiguity we see when we consider *Warning Shadows* in terms of style and genre might well be tied to its content, which brings together multiple strands of cultural discourse that were of real significance at the time. Anton Kaes has emphasized the ways in which films actively intervene in their cultural contexts and "negotiate collective fears, hopes, and hidden anxieties."[6] When we unpack the nesting dolls that we find in *Warning Shadows*, in other words, we find that they are not just components of this odd little narrative, but rather take part in the larger process of shaping German culture in the early 1920s. With filmmakers, critics, and the broad public debating the form that film should take, its relationship to other art forms, and its positioning on the spectrum from "popular" to "high" culture, *Warning Shadows* not only engaged with these questions through its narrative and form, but later also prompted Robison to publicly articulate his ideals of silent film. Its content, too, has to be considered in connection to the specific cultural moment in which it emerged. The entertainment staged by the illusionist—who initially uses his hands to form shadows on the wall, then sets up the "Chinese" shadow play—points not only to the development of cinema, but also to the animated silhouette films that were enjoying so much popularity at the time; the best known of these, Lotte Reiniger's *Die Abenteuer des Prinzen Achmed* (*The Adventures of Prince Achmed*, 1926), was already in production in 1923. And the centrality of hypnosis and of the idea of "experiencing" something in a state of trance was no mere narrative device, but tapped into the fascination with—and anxiety about—the potential power of hypnotism that emerged in Weimar culture. Hypnotism here should be viewed in two ways: as part of a psychological practice that was at least on the way to legitimacy, and as the purview of fairground hucksters and illusionists. Which leads us straight to cinema itself, again: after all, the medium is often conceptualized and bound up with these very concepts. The filmmaker as illusionist, the images on the screen as a sort of dream, a vision, a hallucination: these are central metaphors that we use in looking at film, and the fact that they form the core of Robison's movie is significant. And let us not forget the content of this projection: the negotiation of illicit desire and jealousy and the resolution of dangerous tensions through the staging of a woman's violent abjection. In a historical context in which women were claiming new political and social rights, this certainly is significant.

From the status of film to psychology and hypnosis to the precarious position of increasingly emancipated women: *Warning Shadows*, in touching on so many different discourses that were significant at the time of its release, is a deeply revealing cultural artifact. Indeed, from the vantage point of today, the fact that *Warning Shadows* is still so little known and occupies such a minor spot in the historiography of Weimar cinema speaks to some of the limiting realities of the field. To reconsider the film, to reposition it within the field, and to reconnect it to its historical context, promises a greater and more nuanced understanding of the cultural discourses that were being negotiated in early Weimar cinema.

The Making of the Movie

Warning Shadows begins with a sequence that draws attention to itself, an introduction of the characters that dispenses with any semblance of cinematic realism. The opening shot of the film shows a stage with a shell-shaped prompter's box at its center and a lit candle on the right; a hand reaches out from the box to grab the candle and pull it back out of sight (0:00:45, fig. 1).[7] Only then does the curtain open to reveal a screen immediately behind it and the introduction of characters begin. We first see the shadow of two hands cover the screen as they move together from the bottom to meet at the center; when they move apart again, they reveal "Der Mann" (the husband), Fritz Kortner, whose shadow dissolves into his physical body. Subsequent characters are presented through combinations of their physical bodies, their own shadows, and shadows of the illusionist's hands or of the flirtatious wife. The last of the mansion's inhabitants, the maid, appears briefly and primarily, it seems, to introduce the illusionist: she walks across the stage, then we see the shadow of a man's head on the screen, followed shortly thereafter by the illusionist himself. He climbs out of the prompter's box, still holding the candle and peering after the maid, then turns to the camera and doffs his hat before following her off the stage. The curtain falls.

From the vantage point of today, it might be easy to dismiss this self-consciously theatrical (or cinematic?) opening sequence as odd but perhaps commonplace at the time, yet it was unusual in 1923, too. Even compared to other expressionist films, this opening stands out. A few years earlier, *Caligari* opened on a shot of the lead character, Francis, in conversation with an old man: they may be musing about spirits and apparently supernatural forces, but they do so in a realistic setting (fig. 2).[8] Lupu Pick's *Scherben* (*Shattered*, 1921) opened with a close-up of railroad tracks. Murnau's *Nosferatu* cut from the explanatory text to a long shot of the city setting before cutting to Hutter and, later, his wife Ellen; again, they are introduced in the course of a "natural" and fairly realistic scene. *Warning Shadows*, in contrast, opens with this peculiar sequence that prompted one reviewer to note that "the presentation of the actors is already unique"[9] and that serves less to introduce its characters than it does to remind the viewer that this is a film, however "realistic" the subsequent narrative might be. This is an opening that was far from

Figure 2. The more realistic opening of *The Cabinet of Dr. Caligari*.

the stylistic norm at the time and that raises questions about the way that its makers wanted to position the film.

Warning Shadows marked the fourth time that Artur Robison directed a film. Robison, who was born in the US in 1883 and moved to Germany with his family at the age of seven, was trained as a medical doctor, but soon left the field because he "was irresistibly drawn to the stage."[10] He began his cinematic career as a performer at a German American theater in the US, but returned to Germany after his father's death in 1914 and turned to film, writing three films and directing two of those three for the production company founded by Lu Synd.[11] His next film credits date to a few years later: in 1921, he wrote a screenplay that would be filmed by Martin Hartweg as *Die Finsternis und ihr Eigentum* (*Darkness and Its Possessions*, 1922), before seemingly coming into his own and writing and directing two films that would be released in 1923, *Zwischen Abend und Morgen* (*Between Evening and Morning*) and *Warning Shadows.*

The premise for *Warning Shadows* is usually credited to Albin Grau—the same Albin Grau who had produced and designed sets and costumes for *Nosferatu*; when Grau's Prana-Film company collapsed after Stoker's widow's lawsuit, he soon formed another, Pan-Film Berlin. *Warning Shadows* was the company's first release,[12] with Grau again responsible for art and costume design. While Anton Kaes notes that Grau's first choice as director was actually Friedrich Murnau,[13] the *Nosferatu* director himself, Robison was a likely choice, having just completed *Between Evening and Morning*. That earlier film, subtitled *Der Spuk einer Nacht* (*One Night's Haunting*), focused on two couples torn apart by infidelity, presenting "one terrible night" in which the characters face "real and apparent death and insanity" and "feverish visions" before "a door is torn open and the light of dawn chases away the haunting visions."[14] The striking similarities between this film and *Warning Shadows* suggest how instrumental Robison was in creating the latter. Indeed, one reviewer of *Between Evening and Morning*, writing after having previously reviewed *Warning Shadows*, pronounced Robison "the man who can cinematically realize nocturnal hauntings and visions" and said that "the supernatural, the mystical is his strength."[15]

Not only did Grau and Robison have experience creating the kind of atmosphere that dominates *Warning Shadows*, they also put together an impressive crew and cast. Perhaps most importantly, they enlisted Fritz Arno Wagner, who had worked with Grau on *Nosferatu* and with Robison on *Between Evening and Morning*, as cinematographer. Wagner was already recognized as one of the most important cinematographers of the time; one reviewer emphasized the centrality of his work, calling *Warning Shadows* "a triumph of photography, a fantastical film that is made believable and effective only due to Wagner's superlative artistic achievement."[16] By 1923, Wagner had an impressive résumé that included not only his work on *Nosferatu*, but also, among many films, on Lubitsch's *Madame Dubarry* (*Passion*, 1919) and *Sumurun* (1920) and Lang's *Der müde Tod* (*Destiny*, 1921), and would go on to work on such classics as Pabst's *Die Liebe der Jeanne Ney* (*The Love of Jeanne Ney*, 1927) and Lang's *Spione* (*Spies*, 1928) and *M* (1931).

The cast, too, was not one of unknowns. Indeed, both Alexander Granach, who stars as the illusionist, and Gustav von Wangenheim, who plays the young admirer, had worked with Grau on *Nosferatu*, where they had the respective roles of Knock, the vampire's minion, and Hutter, the protagonist. Granach was an established actor who had started on the stage before moving to the screen; he would continue his prolific work until he was forced to flee Germany in 1933 because of his leftist politics and his Jewish background, and would end up continuing to work once he arrived in Hollywood. Wangenheim's best-known role is surely that of young Hutter, but he, too, was a seasoned actor. Fritz Kortner, who plays the jealous husband, was even better known, with more than one hundred film credits to his name and an equally prolific stage career. Like Granach, both Wangenheim and Kortner would be forced to leave Germany when the Nazis rose to power. Ruth Weyher, who took the part of the wife, was not as well-known as her male colleagues, but would enjoy steady work as an actor throughout the 1920s, including, a few years later, in Pabst's *Secrets of a Soul*, and was famous enough to merit the publication of several chatty autobiographical articles in film journals in 1927 and 1928 (fig. 3).[17] Weyher's career, like that of so many actors from the silent era, seems not to have survived the transition to sound: she had roles in only two sound films, after which her name largely disappeared from trade magazines and other press sources.[18]

Fritz Rasp, who played the younger of the two servants, did so with a convincing malevolence that presaged the trajectory of his career, in which he would figure in everything from Lang's *Metropolis* and *Die Frau im Mond* (*The Woman in the Moon*, 1929) to Pabst's *Tagebuch einer Verlorenen* (*Diary of a Lost Girl*, 1929), often as a similarly antagonistic character. Indeed, given that even Karl Platen, who played the older servant, and the three anonymous admirers (Ferdinand von Alten, Max Gülstorff, and Eugen Rex) have significant credits to their name, the credited cast in its entirety was made up of seasoned and successful actors. Save one, that is: Lilly Harder, who is cast as the maid, doesn't appear to have any other role to her credit.

With its strong cast and production team, *Warning Shadows* was a promising project from the start. And—while it was perhaps not a smash hit—the reviews were generally positive; some were even effusive. It premiered on October 16, 1923 at the Union Theater Nollendorfplatz (fig. 4). This alone should speak to the fact that expectations for *Warning Shadows* were strong: the Union, an imposing, 850-seat movie theater,[19] was no minor venue, but rather one of the famed "palaces of distraction" that Siegfried Kracauer described in a 1926 essay;[20] in fact, it was the first free-standing movie theater built specifically as such. On its opening as the Cines-Theater in 1913, *Der Kinematograph* had described this "new temple

Ruth Weyher:
MEIN LEBEN

Da zu jeder korrekten Lebensbeschreibung die Angabe des Geburtsdatums gehört, will ich es offenbaren, zumal ich glaube, daß ich mir diese Enthüllung noch leisten kann: also ich bin am 28. Mai 1903 in Nowinjasta in Polen als Tochter eines Deutschen und einer Polin zur Welt gekommen. Aber ich war noch sehr winzig, als wir nach Danzig-Langfuhr zogen, wo ich das Lyzeum besuchte und dann meinen Unterricht durch eine Hauslehrerin erhielt. Im Laufe der Jahre wurde schließlich die Berufsfrage aktuell. Als Beamtentochter wird man, wenn man häßlich und fleißig ist, Lehrerin oder Krankenpflegerin, andernfalls kommt man in ein Pensionat oder in die Haushaltungsschule, um sich für die Ehe vorzubereiten. Ich war weder häßlich noch fleißig genug, auch hatte ich zu einem bürgerlichen Beruf keine Lust. Um meine künstlerischen Neigungen in aussichtsreiche Bahnen zu lenken, wurde ich in die Kunstgewerbeschule nach Halle geschickt, studierte gleichzeitig Gesang und gab mein ganzes Taschengeld für Theaterbilletts aus.

Ein Kehlkopfleiden machte dem Singen ein Ende. 1919 kamen wir nach Berlin, und drei Wochen später entdeckte mich in der Stadtbahn Artur Teuber vom Eichberg-Film. Er erklärte mit großer Bestimmtheit, daß man „mit dem Kopp" filmen müsse; nach zwei Tagen erhielt ich eine Aufforderung, mich im Büro einzufinden, und nach einigem Hin und Her wurde mir von meinen Angehörigen die Erlaubnis erteilt, mich vorzustellen. Richard Eichberg und Teuber diskutierten ziemlich lange über „meinen Kopp", schließlich einigte man sich, daß ich in dem neuen Eichberg-Film zusammen mit Lee Parry spielen sollte. Der Anfang war gemacht, aber das Weiterkommen war nicht so einfach, denn ich mußte meinen Weg allein zu finden wissen und hatte niemanden, der mir behilflich war. Erfüllung meiner künstlerischen Sehnsucht war eigentlich das Theater, und ich studierte darum bei Reinhardt. Als ich jedoch mit 200 Mark Monatsgage für das Deutsche Theater engagiert werden sollte, bekam ich von Robert Reinert aus München das Angebot, mit einer Anfangsgage von 2000 Mark im Monat und der Aussicht auf schöne Reisen nach München zu gehen und dort zu filmen. Es war klar, wofür ich mich entschied. Nach Beendigung des Reinertfilms „Sterbende Völker" kam ich nach Berlin und habe so nach und nach in einer großen Reihe sehr schöner Filme gespielt, wie „Komödie des Herzens", „Das Geschöpf", „Die Feuertänzerin", „Geheimnisse einer Seele", „Die keusche Susanne" und zuletzt in „Paname". Den größten Erfolg hatte ich in „Schatten", die größte Freude hat mir die Rolle des Hyppolita im „Sommernachtstraum" gemacht.

Hyppolita
in „Ein Sommernachtstraum"

Als Kind

Die keusche Susanne

In „Paname"

Wenn die Mädchen nah' an
Sechszehn . .

Figure 3. One of several autobiographical articles written by Ruth Weyher.

Figure 4. The Union-Theater Nollendorfplatz. Postcard image from 1913, Wikimedia Commons.

of the arts" as "a peculiar building, with a windowless, yet still elegant and original façade that draws the gaze of passers-by."[21] The venue, therefore, was not merely a large theater, but rather testimony to the transformative power of cinema: in conceptualizing and building theaters like this, architects contributed to the changing urban face, erecting what became landmarks and simultaneously monuments to the growing significance of cinema. This is not to say that, in 1923, the theater, by now re-named Union-Theater am Nollendorfplatz, was *the* top venue in Berlin, but it was certainly important. Four years later, it would be one of the two theaters hosting the opening of Lang's *Metropolis*.[22]

But we remain in October 1923. The day after the premiere, a critic in the *Film-Kurier* praised Robison's movie: "This peculiar, fantastical capriccio was able to strongly hold the attention of a broad audience. The viewers followed the original plot, which, as we know, is based entirely in the unreal, with intense attention, and applauded genuinely at the end. The film, which stands far above the average production, will certainly be viewed with the strongest interest."[23] The Austrian trade journal *Der Filmbote* called *Warning Shadows* "one of the most interesting and promising movies of recent German production,"[24] while the *Kinematographische Monatshefte*, which had previously published a review, dedicated an additional four pages to an analysis of the film, emphasizing that this exceptional action was due to "the significance of *Warning Shadows*, which exceeds that of any German or foreign productions that we have hitherto seen."[25]

Defining Film: Art Form or Public Danger?

This critical acclaim points to Robison's deliberate attempt to make not just a film, but rather an *artistic* film, one that would, as one of the anonymous reviews in *Kinematographische Monatshefte* proclaimed, "strike new paths for German cinema and help to spread its reputation throughout the world."[26] Exemplifying his belief that film, as an exclusively visual medium, should strive to avoid textual components that belong to other art forms like theater, Robison eschewed intertitles in *Warning Shadows*. This not only became a key part of the publicity for the film, with one exemplary advertisement in *Der Kinematograph* announcing that it was "a movie without intertitles" in font far larger than that naming the cast and crew (fig. 5),[27] but also spurred Robison's subsequent involvement in an at-times contentious debate about intertitles that played out in the pages of the *Film-Kurier* a few months after *Warning Shadows* premiered, when one critic dismissed the project of films without intertitles and prompted Robison's ardent rebuttal. At the same time, though Robison might have been the most vocal proponent of moving film in this direction, he was by no means the only one, nor even the first. Rather, the question of whether (and, if so, how) intertitles should be used predates *Warning Shadows*. Indeed, in some ways, we can consider the debate a proxy for the larger questions that

Figure 5. An ad for *Warning Shadows* from the trade journal *Der Kinematograph*.

went to the very heart of cinema: what *was* film actually? Was it merely meaningless mass entertainment, a sort of replacement for "real" culture—like theater—that played to the masses' economic and entertainment needs? Or was it an independent medium that should develop its own norms and techniques? Was it a danger to public morality? Or a potential vehicle for enlightenment?

This anxiety about film goes back to its very roots. Sabine Hake links the apprehension early film engendered to the social and cultural structures fundamental to Wilhelmine Germany and notes that cinema was associated both with "the rising working class and the demand for forms of entertainment appropriate to their working and living conditions" and with "states of psychological and social regression that many thought antithetical to the exigencies of modern society."[28] The links between early film and the working class were in part bound up with its very mode of exhibition. As Joseph Garncarz has shown, from the start, the circumstances of film exhibition shaped the way the medium developed. Until 1905/06, movies were most frequently shown either as part of a larger program in urban variety theaters or by traveling entertainers at the various popular traveling fairs.[29] And, while Garncarz asserts that the latter were the purview not only of the working class, he does emphasize the ways in which the traveling shows in particular cut across social classes and had a much broader appeal than did the more rarified, urban variety shows.[30] When more permanent spaces for movie screenings began to pop up after the "cinema boom" that started in 1905, issues of class entered even more strongly into the medium's development, since most of those early movie theaters, which were essentially no more than converted retail shops and hence called *Ladenkinos* (shop cinemas), catered to the working class.[31]

With even the development of early movie venues exemplifying a sort of vacillation between spheres of low and high (or at least higher) culture, it's no wonder that the development of the medium itself followed a similar trajectory. From the start, film was seen not simply as another artistic medium, but as something inextricably bound up with modernity—and, correspondingly, as something dangerous and in need of regulation; it was simultaneously "a plague" and an "epidemic" and a potential tool for enlightenment that might serve as "the surest treatment for whatever ills modernity had spread."[32] This anxiety about film found its expression in the *Kinoreform* (cinema reform) movement. Part of a larger social reform movement that swept Germany from the end of the nineteenth century up to 1920, the *Kinoreform* movement aimed to regulate film in such a way as to keep those most vulnerable—especially children—safe from its pernicious influence and to redirect its effects in positive ways in order to educate the viewers.[33] The movement's hoped-for reforms varied: proponents decried narrative films as "cinema drama" (*Kinodrama*) that was driven by base capitalism.[34] They saw popular film as failing the task it should serve, a task they couched in aesthetic terms, namely "to record movement and 'real life'. The argument for filmic realism, of course, coincided with their desire to use cinema for educational purposes."[35]

One focus of the *Kinoreform* movement was an anxious preoccupation with the real effects of film venues on physical and psychological health: reformers argued that merely attending movie screenings endangered the viewers, exposing them to a host of threats, such as "the foul air, the passive sitting, the flickering of the images, the unpleasant music, and, most of all, the dubious company."[36] But the movement touched on the relationship between film and art and on aesthetics, as well. Writing in 1913, ten years before the making of *Warning Shadows*, reformer Hermann Häfker saw cinema—specifically narrative cinema—as a dangerous rival of "true" art, luring those longing for the type of experience previously offered by the stage, but offering them only impressions that he saw as diametrically opposed to what they should have been seeking, impressions that "were not 'pure,' but rather appealed to base instincts."[37] In spite of this condemnation of popular film's appeal,

Häfker by no means wanted to see the medium disappear: rather, he recognized its potential power and wanted precisely to reform it in such a way as to maximize its utility. He saw the potential in film to serve a unique purpose, namely "not just to represent 'reality,' but rather specifically that reality that no other technique or artistic medium can represent: that of free, objective movement in nature and all of its rich details."[38] For Häfker, then, film's primary object should be documentary; still, he allowed that some narratives could provide truly artistic material, and his thoughts on this in many ways form a backdrop to Robison's movie, made a decade later: he notes the need to consider the technical possibilities of film, rather than the traditions of the stage, when choosing story and cinematographic approach, and articulates the hope that doing so might lead to developing film as "a new and mature mimetic art."[39] In a statement that carries clear parallels with the ideas that motivate Robison, Häfker ultimately decrees: "Words may under no circumstances disturb gestures, neither as 'explanations' nor as 'dialogue.' If words must play a part, then they must be located between images."[40]

The fact that Häfker, writing a full decade before *Warning Shadows* and from a socio-pedagogic perspective rather than an artistic one, was already articulating a central concern shared by Robison is a reminder that the question of whether or not movies should include text was not simply an aesthetic choice, but rather went to the heart of the medium's status: was it a separate art form, with unique qualities that the filmmaker should abide by, even celebrate? Or was it located between media, a "changeling" that could neither attain the artistic heights of the stage nor develop its own?[41] Could film ever be considered art—and so part of "high" culture—or was it base entertainment, catering to the "masses" and thereby only ever on the fringes of cultural production?

In the years after Häfker staked out these arguments, the debate continued. By the 1920s, German cinema was more established, the film industry was a lucrative business, and movies were no longer screened in often-shabby *Ladenkinos*, but rather in venues that testified to the cultural significance of the medium, the "grand film palaces, which were the most significant and most numerous public building enterprises of the entire Weimar Republic."[42] The *Kino-Debatte*, the ongoing debate "around the cinema's drive to respectability"[43] of which the issues touched on by Häfker are part, had become even more pressing. In May of 1923—a few months before the premiere of *Warning Shadows*—the *Kinematographische Monatshefte* featured a four-page article titled "The Struggle over the Intertitle," whose author, Erich Staude, lamented that discussions about the use of intertitles had hitherto ignored the opinions of average viewers. Staude wanted to rectify this by undertaking a casual survey of viewers to poll their opinions on this heated debate that was clearly invested in far more than the intertitles themselves. Oddly enough, the condemnation of intertitles came from both sides; as Staude noted, the opponents of film saw the use of intertitles as undermining film's claim to art, "since the visual representation of dramatic material cannot do without the disruptive aid of textual explanations," while proponents of film who rejected subtitles did so "passionately and for artistic reasons due to the belief that film can only be a self-contained art once it has overcome and rejected the intertitle."[44] Staude identified how the debate over the intertitle was functionalized as a proxy for a larger discussion about the status of film that gave little weight to the viewers themselves, who "don't question whether there are too many or too few intertitles"— which should not suggest lack of sophistication, since they "have a surprisingly unerring sense for improbable events and unmotivated leaps in the plot."[45]

Though Staude's article did not refer to specific films, there were several made before *Warning Shadows* that purposely used minimal intertitles, specifically Leopold Jessner and Paul Leni's *Hintertreppe* (*Backstairs*, 1921) and Lupu Pick's *Scherben* (*Shattered*, 1921). After *Warning Shadows* premiered in October 1923, two more such films were released: in January 1924, Pick's *Sylvester* (*New Year's Eve*); in December of that year, Murnau's *Der letzte Mann* (*The Last Laugh*). It was shortly after *Sylvester*'s premiere that the debate about intertitles again flared up, this time in the pages of the trade journal *Film-Kurier*, and with Robison representing one side of the argument. The first salvo was fired when Walter Jonas[46] acerbically noted that, "since the release of Carl Mayer's *New Year's Eve*, a ghost that cannot be put to rest is making noise in the German trade press again: the titleless film."[47] Jonas took a clear position against the belief that films without intertitles represent "'the only true film'" and noted that champions of the idea could only justify it negatively, by attempting to differentiate film from literature, theater, and other media. He argued that media are interrelated and that "film, above all, made up of image and written word, is a composite," much like opera and theater. Jonas's article—and especially his tone—was provocative, as he called "the mania of titleless films" typical for Germany, where "overly witty minds limit organic development with their rigid theories and speculation," and pointed damningly and directly to movies that he felt proved the necessity of intertitles: "[Words] cannot be done without. *New Year's Eve* and *The Street* [*Die Straße*, Karl Grune, 1923] are instructive examples of this."

Robison's response, printed a few days later in the same journal, makes clear just how personally he took Jonas's critique: calling Jonas a "currently unemployed ruffian" who showed "aggressive simplemindedness" in attacking his betters, and noting that Jonas's vociferousness was "only exceeded by his creative ineptitude,"[48] he mounted an ardent defense of filmmakers like Mayer and Pick and essentially suggested that Jonas was unqualified to critique their work: "It has an unpleasant effect on one's stomach when a Mr.— what was his name again—a Mr. Jonas can't show more tact and self-awareness towards the bravery of those like Karl Mayer and Lupu Pick than to use them as the cornerstone for the excrement of his reactions."[49] Robison's statement is fascinating not only for its content, but also for the insight it suggests into the filmmaker himself and into the tenor of the conversation about film that was happening at the time. His insistence on the "bravery" of those who created movies without intertitles—Mayer, Pick, and implicitly Robison himself—is evidence not just of his consciousness as an artist and filmmaker, but also of his understanding of the tension between opposing interests—artistic and economic—in cinema. In his fiery polemic, Robison draws a sharp distinction between the taste of "the general masses," which he suggests Jonas represents, and the films he and "a small, heretical minority" are making, films that might "intellectually challenge" Jonas; his disdain for the popular taste represented by Jonas becomes quite evident:

> We can easily believe Mr. Jonas that he would rather satisfy his musical needs with *Madame Butterfly* or even more with *The Merry Widow* than with that terribly useless, textless Ninth Symphony; that he prefers a Reczniceck drawing with its risqué humor to the most beautiful Rembrand [*sic*]; that a plaster of Säckingen's trumpeter with its "God bless you" more deeply touches him than Michel Angelo's [*sic*] *Moses*.[50]

Robison not only suggests that popular taste eschews true art, but also implicitly places himself and others who dare experiment with artistic film firmly among the greats. Certainly, Robison's tone is as condescending and irritating as was Jonas's. A wry editorial comment added in a footnote to Robison's commentary on Beethoven's Ninth is telling: "Psychologically speaking, it's not uninteresting that the author's counterexample [to opera] is the Ninth, which is exceptional in that it does *not* exclude words."[51]

Robison's argument has parallels to the concerns of reformers like Häfker, in that both saw in popular film a form lacking aesthetic value and embodying an uneducated disdain for art; this in spite of the fundamental difference in their aims, with the former idealizing aesthetic achievement and advancement of the specific medial techniques, while the latter wanted to employ film for the purposes of education and representation of reality. At the same time, the pointed commentary by the editors, drawing attention to an instance of the filmmaker's own lack of cultural awareness, suggests impatience with a position that so directly devalues popular cinema. And, while Robison would continue to articulate an interest in films without intertitles, he was himself keenly aware of their limitations. Even as he excoriated Jonas for his position, he noted that "few topics are suitable to pure, wordless filmmaking."[52] *Warning Shadows* may well have raised his profile as a filmmaker, but what Robison gained from this was a contract with Erich Pommer's Universum Film AG, known as Ufa,[53] where he made movies like *Pietro, der Korsar* (*The Love Pirate*, 1925) and *Die Todesschleife* (*Looping the Loop*, 1928), productions that had budgets big enough to allow for filming in exotic locations (Rome for the former, London for the latter) and casting of Ufa stars, that aimed explicitly at a more international market, and that featured intertitles. In his own words, stated after filming *Looping the Loop*, Robison explained:

> My idea is the titleless film, as I see intertitles as a foreign component, a stopgap that must explain that which composition and the visual shot should show. As long as there is a sharp differentiation between the artistic film and popular film, however, the director has to make allowances out of responsibility to the monetary risk of the producer. Thus, the director today can't make a movie that is one hundred percent artistic, but rather at most one that is fifty percent artistic.[54]

Is this an acknowledgement that with *Warning Shadows* Robison had hewed too closely to his aesthetic ideals? Certainly, he takes a different tone here: not abandoning those ideals, but demonstrating an understanding of the financial and structural constraints of the film industry and of the need to take these—as well as, implicitly, the tastes of the audience—into account. And for all its critical acclaim, for all the acknowledgment that it was "a brave attempt at cinematic *l'art pour l'art*,"[55] *Warning Shadows* had not fully realized Robison's goal. Ultimately, the audience seemed to prefer intertitles. A critic in the Viennese trade journal *Der Filmbote* extolled the fact that *Warning Shadows* "is entirely comprehensible even without intertitles, as the successful Berlin premiere, during which there were no intertitles shown, proves," then added laconically: "For the Viennese screenings, intertitles will still be added."[56] That this addition, however much it might undermine Robison's artistic aims, had commercial motivations is evident: one announcement noted that the alteration would "better correspond to the wishes of Vienna's theater owners."[57] The implication is clear: a movie without the customary intertitles posed a much greater financial risk. Artistic statement or not, *Warning Shadows*, it seems, had a better chance at becoming a hit if it conformed to the usual cinematic model.

A Film "Full of Eroticism"

The framing of *Warning Shadows* as an artistic film may well have had an additional benefit, in that it forestalled any real challenge to the content of the film. In her 1952 book *The Haunted Screen*, another of the foundational texts of German film history, Lotte Eisner drew attention to one of the more striking elements of *Warning Shadows* when she noted that it was "full of eroticism, yet there is no vulgarity."[58] Indeed, the sumptuous bedroom and the dining room with its stage-like frame and the emphasis on the "nocturnal" setting serves to amplify an erotic energy that is the heart of the film's content and that is not merely implied, but openly staged: from the wife's seductive dance in front of a candelabra that renders her dress near-transparent to her encounter with her lover in her bedroom to the sexual overtones of her violent murder, the erotic content is surprisingly explicit. Today's viewer might well ask how this aspect of *Warning Shadows* fit into the cinematic landscape of its time: would audiences have seen it as overly risqué? Did censors see no issues with it?

In pragmatic terms, it's notable that the censorship process seems to have been straightforward: two versions of *Warning Shadows* were submitted in July 1923 (one of these with intertitles, presumably in case the version without proved a flop) and were apparently passed with little discussion. Indeed, the fact that *Warning Shadows* was rated *künstlerisch* (artistic) by the censorship board[59] suggests that there was no real objection to its content, however risqué it might seem to the viewer today. One reason for this might be that censorship had effectively been ended by the constitution of the Weimar Republic and, while authorities and reformers tried to regulate the content of films and performances, much of this work focused on the wave of *Aufklärungsfilme* (enlightenment films) that began right around the end of the First World War. Best known today are films like Richard Oswald's *Anders als die Andern* (*Different than the Others*, 1919), a sympathetic depiction of the dangers posed by laws against homosexuality that drew on the scientific work of Magnus Hirschfeld, the founder of the Institut für Sexualwissenschaft (Institute for Sex Science). But while Oswald effectively inaugurated the genre and saw it as a way of educating the populace, other filmmakers took advantage of lax censorship laws, using the purported aim of education to cloak films heavy on titillation, with some 150 such productions made in those early years after the war.[60]

Questionable *Aufklärungsfilme* were only one form of erotic film: long before that genre was born, there were those who saw in the medium the potential for titillation. From the turn of the century on, *pikante Filme* (risqué films) were a popular genre. These were starkly differentiated from outright pornography, in which sexual acts were depicted and which were shown only in private settings like brothels and private homes. *Pikante Filme* focused entirely on the nude female body, presenting short narratives that essentially revolved around striptease.[61] Early on, these films were staples of public cinemas, but as film became ever more established and subject to the pressures not only of authorities, but also of a public liable to brand this kind of entertainment indecent, they, too, increasingly became the purview of private *Herrenabende* (gentlemen's evenings); by 1910, the erotic content shown in public theaters had become much more limited.[62]

Though *pikante Filme* disappeared long before the release of *Warning Shadows*, that history of (mildly) erotic film forms a backdrop to the ways in which erotic content manifested in films produced after the war. With increasing limits on what could be shown in public cinemas, both *Aufklärungsfilme* and those that didn't aspire to "scientific" status framed erotic content less openly than the *pikante Filme* would have. At the same time, the prolonged process of reestablishing some form of censorship in the early years of the Weimar Republic allowed for a certain level of freedom in cultural expression. Even before the war, nudity had been incorporated into artistic performance, with authorities branding it indecent only when sexual acts were performed. The early Weimar era saw the proliferation of performances that today might be deemed scandalous. Celly de Rheydt's *Nakttanz* (naked dance) was a popular attraction from 1919 to 1921;[63] when she was taken to court in 1921 and finally convicted in February 1923, it was only because the nudity in her performances was deemed not artistic, but rather titillating.[64] Anita Berber's stage performances, with titles like "Cocaine" and "Suicide," frequently featured nudity and drew crowds in the early 1920s.[65] And, in 1923, the same year in which *Warning Shadows* was released, Berlin's Komische Oper staged a traveling revue that was titled *Europa spricht davon* (Europe is talking about it) and that was described by a Viennese newspaper as a four-hour production that included skits, comedy performances, singers, and "a hundred-person ballet corps that performs amazing feats not only in dazzling costume, but also in piquant nude dance."[66]

Put in this context, in spite of its focus on desire, infidelity, and jealousy, *Warning Shadows* must have seemed fairly tame, making it less of a target for film censors. And the fact that Robison presented it as an explicitly artistic film might have been one more reason why its content went unchallenged: unlike with Celly de Rheydt's nude dance, one could make the argument that *Warning Shadows* drew on its suggestive elements in support of a clear, artistic narrative. In an odd afterlife, however, the movie was re-released in late 1928 under the title *Die Nacht der Erkenntnis* (*Night of Realization*), billed as "the first recorded lecture film" and promising to reveal the "dangerous awakening of the human psyche's sleeping desire and lust" (fig. 6). Though the inclusion of a lecture suggested an educational film, the lurid poster clearly referenced *Warning Shadows*, but exaggerated the imagery from Robison's original film: the woman is surrounded by creatures who look only half-human, their reaching hands turned into grasping claws. The fact that *Warning Shadows* was recast in this way, as a spectacle promising shocking entertainment that would be, as the poster notes, "only for adults," draws attention again to the erotic content of the original and to how much the framing of the film— on its release in 1923 as an artistic piece, in this (unauthorized) re-invention in 1928 as pseudo-educational—would have determined the interpretation of the erotic content.

Projections within Projections

The narrative proper begins with a long shot of a marketplace at night, a well at its center, and a large mansion with four long, brightly lit windows looming over everything (0:05:00). The illusionist enters the foreground of the frame, sits down briefly at the edge of the steps leading into the square, then rises and descends. The sequence cuts in closer, showing him sit down with his back against the well.

Figure 6. A second incarnation: *Warning Shadows* loses its artistic status. Image source: DFF—Deutsches Filminstitut & Filmmuseum, Frankfurt am Main / Plakatarchiv.

A second, youthful figure enters the space and pauses, his back to the camera. We cut to a medium shot of the two men, the youth in the foreground holding a bouquet and gazing longingly towards the house, the illusionist behind him watching, then to a shot of three

Figure 7. Misleading silhouettes.

of the windows, in one of which we see the silhouette of a couple embracing (0:06:10, fig. 7).

Shortly after this, the sequence cuts from the silhouettes to the figures casting them: at the window inside, the woman pulls herself out of her husband's embrace and gestures him away; once he's gone, we see her pull aside the curtain and look outside. The youth smiles up at what is surely an invitation, while the illusionist looks on.

From the first, the movie shows us what it promises: shadows and silhouettes, and what's more, ones that misrepresent, that pretend to be legible while misleading those who try to read them. The couple silhouetted in the window appears to be a pair of devoted lovers, leaving the young admirer temporarily crushed; in fact, their embrace is one-sided, a means for the wife to send away her husband and invite his rival in. This is only the first of what will be repeated misreadings of appearances. Once the young admirer and the couple's three other guests are inside, the viewing positions are reversed when the husband witnesses what looks like intimate transgression on the part of his wife and their guests. As she preens in front of a mirror, the three admirers notice her shadow falling on the curtained glass panes of the door, then move between it and her, gesturing in such a way that their hands' shadows seem to caress her (0:11:53, fig. 8).

While their actions, however lascivious, are in fact simply play with perspective, the husband, standing outside, sees silhouettes projected on the door that suggest they are actually touching her (0:12:25, fig. 9). Appearance, again, cannot be trusted; perspective determines how it is read. And yet, these shadows and silhouettes set the action in motion, feeding the husband's jealousy until it is expressed in the hallucinated murder.

Shadows that tell stories and suggest meaning: at its heart, this is what film is, as well. Fittingly, the German title of Robison's movie is simply *Schatten*, which would more accurately be translated as *Shadows* than as *Warning Shadows*. As noted, when it was released in Germany and Austria, it was at times given subtitles: the best-known of these is *Eine nächtliche Halluzination* (A Nocturnal Hallucination); for the Austrian market, it was subtitled *Eines Gauklers Spiel* (An Illusionist's Performance); a third subtitle, *Nacht der Erkenntnis* (Night of Realization) was also used in advertising. These multiple titles are fascinating: they simultaneously show producers grappling with how best to explain the actual content of the film and draw attention to the different interpretations of the multiple projections-within-the-projection—and the projection that is the film itself. Hallucination, performance, medium for realization: what exactly is it that the audience sees on screen? The "nocturnal" quality of the "hallucination" suggests that eroticism that could be part of something illicit or risqué, but it serves as well to lead to "realization," or even, if we consider the nuances of the term *Erkenntnis*, to "enlightenment," "discovery," "understanding."

Figure 8. Playing with shadows . . .

Gaukler is also a loaded term, connoting not simply an illusionist, but specifically an itinerant, even potentially dishonest one, and is associated with the notion of "jemandem etwas vorgaukeln," that is, "to deceive someone into believing an untruth." The film's title and its various subtitles thus already suggest slippage between reality and illusion and raise doubts about both the content of the shadows on the screen and the motivations of the one projecting them. The latter, of course, is again ambiguous, even doubled: does the illusionist *on* screen stand in for the one *off* the screen, that is, for Robison himself? Or is the former only another creation of the latter, a false double for the director himself?

The way these different subtitles problematize the status of film as well as that of the filmmaker is fitting, for, at its heart, *Warning*

Figure 9. . . . and reading shadows wrong.

Shadows can be viewed as a film about film, with its narrative centering not only the shadows, reflections, and distortions that stand in symbolically for the medium, but also the medial precursors of film, such as shadowgraphy and the silhouette play. Shadows themselves occupy a peculiar position in a world that we view as "real." As E. H. Gombrich notes: "They are not part of the real world. We cannot touch them or grasp them and so ordinary parlance often resorts to the metaphor of shadows to describe anything unreal."[67] Little wonder why film has so long been characterized as, in Maxim Gorky's words, "the Kingdom of Shadows"[68]: all we see on the screen before us cannot be grasped, does not have the "reality" of the world around us. Expanding on this and pointing to the ways in which shadows function in film, Victor Stoichita argues that they show us "what is taking place *inside* the character, what the person *is*," and points to *Nosferatu* as revealing the close relationship between shadow and medium: "The function of the director is in effect that of a 'shadow-master'. He portrays the dark contents of the mind and turns them into a story that is, to all appearances, an aesthetic that accentuates the analogy between 'shadow' and 'cinematic image.'"[69]

Stoichita's analysis of *Nosferatu* is not only strikingly pertinent to *Warning Shadows*, but also suggest that there are more connections between the two films than shared cast and crew. Anton Kaes reads *Nosferatu* as in many ways being a film about film: a film, that is, that draws into question the distinction between the real and the "shadows," between conscious and unconscious. Since everything on the screen is constructed—is, in effect, nothing but shadows— it becomes impossible to clearly delineate "between reality and hallucination."[70] We see that same ambiguity in *Warning Shadows*: shadows, silhouettes, and reflections occupy a liminal space and are simultaneously dangerously real and reassuringly intangible. Like film itself, the shadows we see are, in the end, performing a fiction, and yet they hold the potential of intervening in a concrete way in the characters'—and the viewers'?—lives, of effecting actual change.

To be sure, the shadow as symbol has a history that long precedes the advent of cinema. In Plato's allegory of the cave, shadows represent the limits of human understanding, the projections taken as real by those who cannot grasp the larger truth behind appearance. In German culture, shadows and doubles occupy a privileged position in Romantic literature: from Chamisso's *Peter Schlemihl* (1813), in which a young man sells his shadow to the devil and finds himself ostracized, to E. T. A. Hoffmann's "Die Geschichte vom verlorenen Spiegelbild" ("The Story of the Lost Reflection," 1815), where a man gives up his reflection for love, Romantic literature again and again turned to the topic. In some ways, the appearance of the motif in early German film points back to that cultural heritage. For example, the very first art film, *Der Student von Prag* (*The Student of Prague*,

Stellan Rye, 1913), tells a story that resonates with its Romantic forebears, that of Balduin, who sells his reflection with fatal results; it proved so compelling a tale that it was remade twice, by Henrik Galeen in 1926 and by none other than Artur Robison in 1935. Katharina Loew argues that one of Rye's goals lay in exploiting those qualities of film that were unique to the medium, and suggests that *The Student of Prague* "prefigured what would become the guiding principle for German artistic filmmaking, namely, as art director Walter Reimann formulated it in 1926, 'to translate the mental into the purely optical.'"[71] In other words, films like *Warning Shadows* not only take part in a process of grappling with cinema's possibilities of representation, but do so in a way that reveals a broader questioning of reality that is bound up with the medium.

Shadows and reflections are thus tied to the ways that both film and the psyche are imagined, and the centering of these motifs certainly befits the cultural context into which *Warning Shadows* was released, one that was grappling with the mystery of the human psyche. The shadows that populate the film, however, are only one motif that resonates with dominant cultural discourses during the early decades of cinema: the central hallucinatory episode, framed as the result of the illusionist's hypnotic powers, connects to a fascination with and investigation of magic, hypnosis, trance states, even the occult as a larger field that forms another part of *Warning Shadows'* background. Reading the character of the illusionist and his powers as being in dialogue with that discursive background sheds more light on what the film reveals about its historical context and its own status as film.

The Illusionist: Magic, Control, and Art

In the unusual introduction that we've already touched on, the first character that we see—though we might not immediately realize it—is the illusionist: his hand reaches out to take the candle; later, he climbs out of the prompter's box from which he's been directing the introduction and into the action of the film, pausing to acknowledge the audience before he chases after the alluring maid. The illusionist, in other words, is the figure around which the narrative as a whole circulates: simultaneously inside and outside the story, orchestrating but equally implicated in it, this opening positions him as both master of ceremonies and part of the action. This dual role is itself doubled: just as he directs the entertainment for the characters within the story even while taking an active part, he serves a double function for the viewers of the film, being both an on-screen image and, as he suggests when he breaches the fourth wall with his literal nod to the audience, a stand-in for the multiple sources of these images who reminds the viewer not only of his function as "projector" of multiple shadow plays, but also of the camera itself and of the theater projection system. However shabby he appears, he has an impressive bag of tricks: from the performance for the servants, in which he casts simple hand-shadow animals on the wall, to the artistically impressive silhouette puppet play or *ombres françaises* to the complicated hypnotic trance, the illusionist leaves his audiences quite literally spellbound. His representation—as purveyor of shadowgraphy, as prestidigitator, as illusionist—draws attention to the connection between cinema and other forms of illusion and sleight of hand.

The illusionist's art is what opens doors for him. He first insinuates himself into the house by trying to convince the older servant of his skills, showing off his carpet bag enticingly (0:19:07). When he notices the maid, he follows her and even dares to touch her legs (0:19:45), leading the servants to drag him away, but he uses his skills to gain freedom: as their shadows loom on a blank wall, he manages to shake them off, steps out of sight behind a wall that serves as a frame within the frame of the shot, then begins to cast his animal shadows for the maid and the servants. The larger-than-life shadows that he projects hold the attention of the servants, who interact with them as with real animals: one reaches a finger towards what looks like a camel's head (0:20:20, fig. 10), then recoils when the shadow snaps at him; both shrink from the shadow of a wolf.

When the younger servant, less impressed, again orders him out, the illusionist demonstrates a second skill: kneeling in front of the wall, he uses cardboard cutouts and his fingers to form two faces that move closer before beginning to kiss (0:21:10, fig. 11).

The servants are so distracted that they ignore the bell rung by the husband to summon them, leading him to join them and try to oust the illusionist. Yet, again, art serves to mesmerize: we see the illusionist raise his hands to form a silhouette of what appears to be a woman, then the sequence cuts to a shot of the wall, the husband's shadow facing the one formed by the illusionist's hands; slowly, the shadow shifts until it looks like the husband's double. Man and shadow-double eye each other (0:22:55, fig. 12) before the sequence cuts back to the group. For a moment, the husband looks unsettled, then he gestures, inviting the illusionist to follow him (0:23:07). The shadowgraphy has worked its magic.

And magic is precisely what is suggested by the effect of the illusionist's performance: it is a magician's performance of illusion, where that illusion is bound up with projection, even with film itself. Erik Barnouw has explored the connections between early film and magicians' performances. Examining the magician's frequent reliance on and integration of the same technical and scientific advances that were the precursors of film, he notes how prevalent the use of the magic lantern was beginning in the late eighteenth century, when it was built into magic shows "covertly for spectacular effect."[72] For illusionists accustomed to using projections in their acts, the advent of film offered a (brief) moment in which they could be on the forefront of the medium's advance. Barnouw traces how inextricably the development of early cinema was bound up with magicians and illusionists who took advantage of the different projection systems that were becoming available in order to continue to lure audiences eager to see magic, this time of the cinematic sort. In the earliest

Figure 10. The illusionist's skills: shadowgraphy ...

Figure 11. ... and more shadow-play.

Figure 12. The husband and his shadow-double.

days of cinema, magicians could simply integrate short films which would themselves strike the audience as magical.[73] Later, they would incorporate films of magic acts; eventually, they would not simply film their usual act, but draw on cinematic tools to increase its impact, a development that inaugurated the early trick film.[74] To be sure, that same medium that magicians embraced so enthusiastically was their undoing: film allowed anyone to duplicate the "sensational illusions" that had populated the magic show, and, in the end, flesh-and-blood performances could not compete with the magic on screen: "The sensations ceased to be sensational. Even on stage they began to seem stale. The magician found he had been helping to destroy his own profession."[75]

Returning to *Warning Shadows*, Barnouw's analysis reminds us that magic and illusion were bound up with the technological advancements that gave birth to cinema. In Robison's film, the illusionist's magic is projection (and vice versa): with only a source of light and first his hands, then the bodies of those around him, he creates the illusion of life on a screen—creates, in other words, a form of cinema—and reminds the viewer of film's very roots. His virtuosity with the different forms of shadow play hearkens back to one of the magicians Barnouw mentions, Félicien Trewey (1848–1920). Trewey rose to fame as an entertainer who excelled at all manners of prestidigitation and illusion, but is perhaps best remembered for his shadowgraphy: after achieving enormous fame with this in his native France, he toured Europe, delighting audiences with intricate shadow plays that went far beyond the kinds of simple projections of animal heads that one commonly associates with shadow play, instead including "not only heads and animated physiognomies, but also full bodies and entire scenes taken from real life."[76] Trewey's fame as magician and illusionist led to his direct involvement in cinema: already famous across Europe, he would take the Lumière Brothers' Cinématographe to London and, from there, across the United Kingdom. Barnouw poses the question of whether Louis Lumière tasked Trewey with this because he saw the Cinématographe as fundamentally akin to the kinds of wonders Trewey staged, something "that would amaze people for a few years and then gradually fade away" or as a medium that was "the ultimate development of shadowgraphy."[77] In either case, Trewey, with his fame as shadowgrapher and illusionist, would be the perfect choice to "direct" the demonstrations. Indeed, he also featured in his films, at times recording his performances before audiences, then showing them those same films, allowing them to experience the *mise en abyme* of the film-within-the-film even at this early stage in cinematic development.[78]

To draw a link between Trewey and the illusionist in *Warning Shadows* might seem tenuous, but Trewey was certainly famous in Germany during his heyday: as the *Berliner Börsenzeitung* reported in 1881, he had to call himself "the Original Trewey" due to the many imitators that tried to take his name.[79] And ultimately, whether or not Robison knew of Trewey in particular, he was one of many similar performers whose acts combined illusion, prestidigitation, and, eventually, film. Like Trewey, the illusionist in *Warning Shadows* presents virtuoso performances of all manner of shadow play; again like Trewey, he both directs and plays a part in his illusions; and in yet another similarity, he stages, for the characters in the film who become an audience, a filmic rendition of their own selves. He hearkens to an earlier time: one in which magicians and illusionists not only populated stages and draw enthusiastic audiences, but also assisted in the birth of film itself. At the same time, he is a figure that points forward to those who had, by the 1920s, taken the place of the earlier illusionists: to film directors themselves. Tom Gunning traces the development of projection from its use in the early phantasmagoria shows to cinema itself, noting that "[t]he phantasmagoria (like the movie projection system that ultimately derived from it) created its illusions primarily by concealing its means of projection."[80] In *Warning Shadows*, too, we see the illusionist work not only with visible tools, like the candle and the paper puppets with which he mounts the Chinese shadow play, but also without: in the hallucinatory episode, he himself disappears, fading out and concealing all evidence of the means of projection and thereby, paradoxically, reminding us yet again of his own position. If the illusionist stands in for Robison, then the connection to this tradition of magic performances—and the various moments in which we not only witness his illusions, but also become privy to how they are created and how easily they may be understood—serves as a winking reminder to us that film, too, is not a representation of reality.

Spectators Become Actors

The illusionist's shadowgraphy might well be impressive, but it is only the first of his illusions. When the husband brings him in to perform for his wife and guests, the illusionist springs into action. Even before he begins his performance proper, he demonstrates the potential danger in his art: as the wife dances flirtatiously in front of her guests, he holds the lit candelabra behind her, making the fabric of her dress appear sheer enough to reveal the silhouette of her legs in a decidedly risqué way (0:26:00, fig. 13).

When the guests react with enthusiasm and the husband with jealous anger, the illusionist stops, but only temporarily. Soon, the guests are seated along one side of the long table, facing a white

Figure 13. A risqué dance.

Figure 14. Deceptive shadows.

canvas that the servants have fastened to the wall. The illusionist crouches to one side of them, sets up a candle on a chair, and begins his performance: a dragon's silhouette appears before we see the projection of a detailed and Orientalist shadow play (0:31:55). But the shadows cast by his audience are as meaningful as those on the canvas, and the illusionist is as much director of the former as of the latter. We see the hand of the wife moving dangerously close to that of her young admirer seated next to her: he adjusts the light source just long enough to project a shadow that seems to show them touching (0:34:38, fig. 14), but when the husband rushes to investigate, he discovers nothing. Perspective and the machinations of the illusionist have again shaped the interpretation of this moment in a way that is entirely different from its actual significance.

And still, all of this is only the preface to the real illusion. As the group laughs half-heartedly, as though to suggest that the husband's jealousy is unfounded, the illusionist puts a candle on the table, asks them all to turn and look at their shadows on the ground behind them (0:35:54, fig. 15), then gestures as though drawing the shadows to the other side. The figures fade out even as they fade in on the other side of the table, seated opposite their original seats (0:36:18, fig. 16). Positioned in front of the canvas, they are now essentially on screen. Stunned for a moment, they seem to wake up. The illusionist is nowhere to be seen: his real performance has begun.

This is the start of the interior story, which we can conceive of variously as hallucination, as trance-like state, as vision, perhaps even as supernatural experience. The content of this hallucinatory episode

Figure 15. The real illusion begins.

Figure 16. The spectators become shadow-actors.

forms the substance of the film as a whole: the wife and the youth flirt openly, the lecherous admirers conspire to distract the husband when the couple sneaks away, the husband's jealousy escalates into murderous rage, and the servants take part in the punishment of the wife—the younger one with clear enjoyment, the older grudgingly. The wife becomes the visual object that centers the sequence: first openly displaying her erotic power, then being made to pay for the same. The rest of the film in some ways seems to serve only to anchor this episode and to justify the content by establishing it as "fantasy" within the film.

The form of the episode is just as important as its content. The iconography used to introduce it references hypnotism, a fact that would have been doubly striking at the time of the film's release, when there was enormous interest in hypnosis, both as legitimate medico-scientific process and as public spectacle. That interest was certainly not new, but it took on new significance in the years after the First World War, a fact that we see reflected broadly in film. As one article noted in 1919: "All tendencies that dominate public life are taken up by film production and mirrored in a thousand variations. If you walk through the streets today, posters for 'seances' call out to you from all the advertising pillars: telepathic ones, hypnotic, suggestive; different words for the same idea."[81] The saturation implied by the advertisements that so dominated the city's visual space speaks to a thirst for the kinds of unconscious or uncanny experiences seances offered, and cinema, too, aimed to quench that thirst. Films now considered classics of the era drew directly or indirectly on the theme of hypnosis: Wiene's *The Cabinet of Dr. Caligari* had a carnival huckster hypnotically controlling the murderous somnambulist; Lang's two-part *Dr. Mabuse, der Spieler* (*Dr. Mabuse, the Player*, 1922) ascribed hypnotic powers to the eponymous archcriminal; even *Nosferatu* suggested that some such power was what drew Ellen to the vampire (and vice versa?). So-called *Kulturfilme*, "cultural films" or documentaries, took on the topic as well. In 1920, the *Neue Kino-Rundschau* described a short film, *Hypnose und ihre Erscheinungen* (*Hypnosis and Its Phenomena*, Thomalla/Rutkowski, 1920), that demonstrated hypnotic experiments and extolled the details that the close-ups used in the film allowed the viewer to see.[82]

While this short documentary from 1920 might have appealed most to a professional audience, one of its directors, Dr. Curt Thomalla, directed a longer film focusing on hypnosis a few years later. *Ein Blick in die Tiefen der Seele* (*A Look into the Depths of the Soul*, 1923), as an unsigned article in *Der Film-Bote* noted, would have to be accompanied by a lecture reminding viewers that, though the film would "open the viewer's eyes and enlighten and stimulate," one should not make the mistake after watching it to "imagine that one has mastered the material."[83] This warning is telling: on one hand, it reveals just how suspiciously authorities viewed hypnosis, requiring any demonstration thereof to be framed scientifically; on the other, it acknowledges that the audience would not be made up of experts, but of viewers searching both for *Aufklärung*, enlightenment, and entertainment. That *A Look into the Depths of the Soul* was a film by the Kultur-Film A.-G., a production company that was part of the Dafu (Deutsch-amerikanische Film-Union A.G.), is an interesting side note, as Dafu also distributed *Warning Shadows*. Whether that link is purely coincidental or not, it suggests how pervasive the interest in hypnosis was: if coincidence, then that would suggest a true proliferation of works about hypnosis; if not, then Dafu seems to have banked on the topic as one that would appeal to viewers.

Hypnotism: Therapy and Spectacle

Hypnosis started out as "mesmerism," named after Fritz Anton Mesmer (1734–1815), who, after completing a medical degree in Vienna in 1766, developed a theory connecting his own ideas about a sort of magnetic fluid or force fundamental to life with the practice of using magnets in healing. To the alarm of the medical establishment, which disdained his work, Mesmer's healing practice, based on what he termed "animalischer Magnetismus" (animal magnetism) and using magnets and his own touch to ostensibly balance the magnetic fluid in the body, became ever more successful in Vienna. When an investigation of his methods was made, it branded his practice "a public menace," but Mesmer refused to comply with the demand to cease his work.[84] Instead, he moved to Paris and set up a clinic that catered to the elite, using techniques that were fundamentally performative ones. Maria Tatar notes that the setting "seemed designed to foster an aura of mystery and magical enchantment," with Mesmer "in a violet robe of embroidered silk and [carrying] with him a magnetized iron wand," a true "master of ceremonies" in these treatments.[85]

Mesmer's methodology seems far removed from the medical use of hypnosis that would develop in the late nineteenth and early twentieth century, but, as Tatar has traced, the approaches that he and his followers used prefigure later work in psychoanalysis, with Mesmer's reliance on generating in his patients "crises and convulsions that allowed [them] to abreact the symptoms of their disease" and his follower Puységur's "interrogation of patients during magnetic sleep [figuring] as the crude antecedents of the cathartic method and the 'talking cure' employed by Breuer and Freud to relieve the symptoms of hysteria."[86] And, clearly, the ambiguity of Mesmer's position—the contempt shown him by the medical field in the face of the enthusiasm of his followers and patients—presages the ways in which hypnotism, too, would be alternately hailed as medical breakthrough and condemned as dangerous trickery.

What was known as mesmerism was eventually renamed hypnotism[87] and continued to develop as a legitimate therapeutic practice in tension and conflict with more popular forms of the process. Outside of medicine, hypnotism was part of a broader field of the occult, spiritualism, and mysticism that drew much interest and was often performed as popular spectacle by traveling hypnotists at various fairs and festivals.[88] The representation of *Warning Shadows*'s traveling illusionist, his box of tricks including everything from simple shadow play to the ability to exert control over his subjects' minds, certainly resonates with these less "respectable" predecessors. To be sure, for those eager to use hypnosis in legitimate ways, these illusionists were often simultaneously a source of inspiration and a distinct threat that solidified the association of the practice with entertainment and trickery.[89]

In medicine, Jean-Martin Charcot at the Salpêtrière in Paris and Hippolyte Bernheim in Nancy were instrumental in shaping the understanding of hypnosis. Charcot is perhaps the better known of the two French physicians, not least for the showman-like theatricality with which he demonstrated his work in "packed lecture halls . . . before international medical and lay audiences" for whom he offered up demonstrations of "symptoms of hysteria, including contractures, tics and convulsions in the bodies of his predominantly female subjects."[90] Indeed, Charcot viewed hypnosis as fundamentally performative: for him hypnosis was not a therapeutic tool, but rather a way of identifying "the hysteric"—since he believed that only those with a predisposition to that malady could be hypnotized—and of displaying hysterical symptoms to the attendees of his lectures.[91] To this end, Charcot not only induced his patients to perform their symptoms before a live audience, but also documented these photographically, and published the photos in his *Iconographie photographique de la Salpêtrière* (Photographic iconography of the Salpêtrière). That the women he treated and hypnotized should themselves effectively become actors in a scene he directed links hypnotism with spectacle, illusion, theater, and, by extension, with cinema itself in a troubling way.[92]

In contrast to Charcot, Bernheim believed hypnosis to be based on suggestion and to have therapeutic value; he felt that Charcot's patients were so strongly under their doctor's influence that their performances were "simply conforming to [Charcot's] ideas rather than illustrating the immutable hysteric states."[93] To Bernheim, anyone could be hypnotized, and the process could serve to enable both psychic and physical healing. Bernheim's approach lacked the straightforward appeal to performance that we saw in Charcot's, and yet his emphasis on hypnosis and suggestion as something that could be applied broadly, to any person, opened up the process in a way that allows us to tie it more directly, as I will discuss later, to cinema.

But first, we linger for a few moments in the late nineteenth century, as hypnosis was developing into a spectacle even in the medical field. Charcot and Bernheim's work made waves outside of France, drawing doctors to observe their work; indeed, when Freud spent several months studying with Charcot, it was a critical experience, spurring him to shift his focus from neurology to psychopathology; for a time, at least, he too believed hypnotism to be a key tool for treatment.[94] And yet, though both Charcot and Bernheim saw hypnotism as a medical technique, and others in the field came to watch and learn from them, the process couldn't quite shake its unsavory reputation. Perhaps this is one reason why hypnotism fell out of fashion among physicians through the turn of the century. Doctors weighed its benefits against potentially dire results. An article describing an 1895 demonstration of hypnotism as a treatment for a young man experiencing paralysis in his right arm noted various expert observers' skepticism: one was convinced of the process's effect, but insisted on the danger of more broad use of hypnotism, seeing it as an infringement on self-determination and noting that it carries "the potential of leading to insanity"; another noted that the demonstration seemed like "conscious playacting," perhaps because the patient not only performed actions proving that his symptoms were alleviated, but also, in a demonstration of posthypnotic suggestion, addressed and conversed with his absent mother.[95] Another article sketched the potential dangers in truly lurid tones, noting that the subject is rendered entirely helpless to the control of the hypnotizer and would even commit "the worst crime" if so ordered, and warning that hypnotizing even "young and healthy individuals" could cause the "temporary derangement which is peculiar to hypnosis to increase with every instance and even become permanent."[96]

The public's continuing fascination with hypnotism in spite (or because?) of its myriad dangers suggests not just an interest in the performance of the act, but also some awareness of its history and process. For example, the speaker at a public lecture in Linz, Austria in 1895 defined hypnosis, sketched out its history from Mesmer to contemporary developments, noted how hypnotism works, and then touched on the differences between subjects who remember the experience and those who don't. The event, which seems to have been predominantly scientific, was a rousing success: the speaker "earned the liveliest applause" and the lecture "may have been one of the best-attended of the season."[97] If these types of events drew such impressive audiences, then the public surely had a fairly strong understanding of hypnotism.

Still, the average person was likely most fascinated not by hypnotism's applicability to psychiatric treatment, but rather by its titillating and terrifying potential: the play with control it implied; the notion that the self could be held in thrall by another. To combat this potential scourge, some countries and localities, including France, Austria, and Italy, enacted laws in the late nineteenth century making the performance of hypnotism by laymen illegal.[98] But these laws could only do so much. Medicine may have turned away from hypnotism around the turn of the twentieth century, but the practice never entirely disappeared and, soon enough, it would again gain traction: during the First World War, it came to be seen as a viable treatment for what was termed *Kriegsneurose*, war neurosis. In Germany, Max Nonne began treating soldiers who presented with symptoms that resembled those of hysterical patients by hypnotizing them. Lerner details how Nonne's public demonstrations, in which he alleviated his patients' symptoms, built his reputation for having "miraculous therapeutic power" and being a sort of "magical healer" or *Zauberheiler*.[99] And yet, again, the revival of interest in the medical use of hypnosis was tied to its reappearance as public spectacle, and the evocation of a sort of magical dimension to Nonne's work suggests that it was seen as not fully scientific. Outside of medicine, legal prohibitions against hypnotism as entertainment simply led its practitioners to hide behind alternate language, as a newspaper summary of a 1920 report prepared for the Berlin police headquarters detailed: "Since public displays of hypnotism are not allowed, organizers talk about psychic experiments, suggestion, conscious and unconscious influences, expeditions into the enigmatic realm of the psyche, animal magnetism, influencing of the will, and so forth."[100] And again, with the renewed interest in hypnotism in medicine and in public life more broadly that arose in these years during and after World War I, new discourses arose around the topic. One question that troubled medicine, law, and literature, for example, was whether crimes could be committed under the influence of hypnotism;[101] newspaper articles enumerated examples of supposed crimes committed either by or against those hypnotized, and the justice system considered in detail whether hypnotism could be used in trials.[102]

What does it mean that *Warning Shadows* explicitly referenced these cultural discourses that represented hypnotism as both potential medical advance and public endangerment, staging the process as part of a film that aimed to be both art and entertainment? Certainly, the pervasiveness of these discourses and the simultaneous fascination and anxiety they elicited from the public forms an important backdrop to the film and promises to shed light on the ways in which audiences at the time would have received the film.

"This Magical Therapy"

Once the couple and their guests fall into the hypnotic sleep, the inhibitions that previously kept their desires and emotions restrained—if barely!—fall away. As they "wake" to their hallucinatory experience (0:36:30), they soon let their urges take over. The wife leans over the youth and teasingly pretends to feed a bite of food to two of her admirers; the youth embraces her waist as she does so (0:36:58, fig. 17); the third admirer, seated on her other side, kisses her arm and eventually makes one strap of her dress fall down.

Covering her chest with her hands, she slowly moves around the table, looks back meaningfully, then leaves the room. As she hesitates outside the door, eyes closed and chest heaving, her three admirers distract her husband so that the youth can follow her (0:39:33). He pauses in the hallway outside her bedroom, and we see her, reflected in the mirror at the rear of the frame, as she opens the door (0:40:12).

Figure 17. Acting on desires.

The sequence cuts to a long shot of her room as she stands at its center in front of her bed, eyes closed. The youth enters and slowly joins her, then the long shot dissolves to a medium shot of them as the woman turns towards the youth, opens her eyes, and they embrace (0:41:00). The depiction of this intimate episode is repeatedly interrupted by cuts to the husband, who shakes off his other guests and leaves them to pursue his wife. He lingers in the hallway outside her room as the youth did earlier, and we see a long shot of him facing the rear of the frame, where he sees the adulterous couple's silhouette on her door reflected in a mirror (0:42:20, fig. 18).

He stares at the mirror, in which their silhouettes give way to the reflection of the youth as he opens the door and steps out of the room (0:42:49, fig. 19) and finally to the reflection of the couple as they kiss passionately (0:42:52, fig. 20).

Figure 18. Another revealing shadow . . .

Figure 19. . . . but this time less innocent.

Figure 20. The reflection in the mirror as proof.

If we consider the events of the trance, we can locate two focal points; this encounter between the wife and the youth (who here becomes her lover, if only in this shadow-state) is the first of them. The sequence complicates our understanding of the events in several ways. On one hand, we see proof of the wife's adulterous desire: her open physical flirtation with the guests carries none of the ambiguity of her earlier actions, and, of course, we see her and the youth in her bedroom. We might, in that moment, still tenuously read her actions as largely innocent, since our view of events is interrupted by a cut to her husband and the other guests, and we see only the initial embrace of the wife and the youth, then return to them as she sits down on a divan and he falls at her knees, his head on her lap. But any ambiguity seems to be removed when we see them kiss in the mirror; indeed, the moment might even push us to retroactively question her actions before the hallucinatory episode. After all, if the intimacy implied by the silhouettes embracing here is proven correct when we see the couple embrace, does this serve to cast doubt on the earlier, parallel moment, in which the husband misinterpreted his wife's silhouette on the other door? In that moment, we saw how appearance belied what was actually happening—but does this episode undermine our earlier belief in the wife's innocence? Or is this sequence no less certain than the previous one? After all, the way in which we witness the wife's infidelity is multiply removed: we see the silhouettes in what we later realize is actually a mirror. Does the fact that, again, we are seeing silhouettes and reflections remind us not to trust this any more than we did the previous shadow plays?

This encounter between the wife and the youth, where she acts on her active desire and vanity, is one focal point of the hallucinatory episode; the second is the depiction of the sadistic punishment to which she is subjected, motivated by her husband's jealousy. First, we see a drawn-out sequence in which the husband prepares his revenge, cross-cutting between the youth as he rejoins the group in the dining room and the husband as he finds a rope and orders his servants to get his wife. While the other men confer with the youth, the husband goes to his study and selects several swords. The wife, exiting her room, pauses in front of a mirror in the hallway, her expression rapturous. It's here that she's interrupted by the younger of the two servants (0:47:53). In a series of medium and long shots, cross-cut with shots of the guests, we watch them struggle: she shakes him off and flees downstairs, only to find herself trapped by a locked door. A masked close-up shows her terrified face, then we cut to a long shot of the hallway: the shadow of her struggling as the servant restrains her moves into the frame; she turns away from him, then he reaches out a hand to cover her mouth (0:49:14, fig. 21).

Still the chase continues: she tears herself away and ducks into an alcove, exhausted, only to find herself trapped again. We see another

Figure 21. Trying to escape.

close-up of her face as her expression changes to terror, then cut to a long shot as she stares down at the shadows that advance and eventually cover her (0:50:33, fig. 22). The servants have found her again, and though she first struggles, then begs, she ends defeated, slumping on the ground.

It's striking how much time is given to these moments before the wife is dragged back to her husband: by the time she is tied down on the table in front of the men, we've watched her go from hopeful that she might be saved by her lover to resigned when he succumbs to the threats of her husband (0:56:50). We see her shadow as the servant ties her down, her body hidden from view by her husband (0:58:02, fig. 23); we see one more struggle as the youth is beaten back by the husband and the admirers obey the command to pick

Figure 22. Trapped.

up their respective swords (1:00:53); we see in close-up as the wife struggles to evade the swords moving towards her (1:01:23); finally, we see her shadow projected onto the wall as three swords pierce her chest (1:01:28, fig. 24).

Once she is dead, the sequence cuts to a long shot of the room, with the table at the center, the wife's body sprawled across it and her head hanging down, facing the camera. In the aftermath of the murder, the husband, crazed by his actions, gets flowers from the garden, but when he returns to put them on her body, the other men finally take action. They push him towards the window and the sequence cuts to a shot from outside, first of their struggling silhouettes on the curtain, then of the window opening. We cut to a long shot as the husband falls to the ground below, then to

Figure 23. Her body on display.

Figure 24. A performance of murder.

Figure 25. The show is over.

a medium shot of his lifeless body on the cobblestones (1:11:22). Here the hallucination ends: the body fades out, leaving the ground empty, and we cut once more inside to a long shot of the other men gathered around the window before the camera tracks out to reveal that the long shot is actually projected on the wall, with the couple and their guests seated in front of it, their backs to the camera (1:11:50, fig. 25).

The screen on the wall fades to white. The illusionist reappears— fading into view against a previously blank wall, then stepping forward to the table, where the others sit as though frozen. We see him in the same high-angle shot as at the outset of the hallucination: this time, he gestures as though pushing their shadows back to their original positions behind them. As he watches, they wake up: he

Figure 26. Breaking the spell.

looks at them, then draws his hand across his forehead as though to suggest that a hallucination is being cleared away (1:13:10, fig. 26). The group is released from his spell.

What does it mean that the central episode of *Warning Shadows* is presented as a hypnotic hallucination? The public interest in hypnotism and the pervasiveness of representations and discussions of the process suggest that viewers would have recognized their connection to the characters' experience; how would that have affected their reading of the film? How *should* it affect *our* interpretation, if at all? On one hand, the use of hypnotism links the film's hallucinated episode to therapy; at the same time, we need to consider how it serves the film's purpose as entertainment, especially in shaping the interpretation of the hallucination's content.

In his seminal work *From Caligari to Hitler*, published in 1947, Siegfried Kracauer had high praise for *Warning Shadows*, suggesting that it was one of only two movies of its era that "aimed at endowing rational thinking with executive powers," even hinting that, had it been successful in this goal, it might have so fundamentally changed German culture as to let reason triumph over what he saw as the collective "dark inhibitions and unchecked impulses" that would end in the horrors of the Nazi regime.[103] Kracauer counts *Warning Shadows* among what he terms "instinct films," those that focus on "the surge of disorderly lusts and impulses in a chaotic world,"[104] and reads the film's narrative as representing a therapeutic treatment undertaken by the illusionist, a "sagacious wizard" who sends the characters "into the realm of the unconscious" where their instincts lead to a catastrophe that serves as treatment:[105]

> The hallucination ends with the furious courtiers throwing the count out of the window.[106] Then the scene shifts back to the hypnotized party alongside the table, and the shadows are seen returning to their owners, who slowly awaken from their collective nightmare. They are cured. White magic has enabled them to grasp the hidden springs and terrible issue of their present existence. Owing to this magical therapy— it recalls model cases of psychoanalytical treatment—the count changes from a puerile berserk into a composed adult, his coquettish wife becomes his loving wife, and the Lover takes silent leave.[107]

The language that Kracauer uses is fascinating: on the one hand, the hallucinatory episode serves a therapeutic function analogous to psychoanalysis and resulting in measurable changes in the characters: initially acting with "the immaturity of instinct-possessed beings,"[108] they awaken "cured" of jealousy, lust, and infidelity. The illusionist has become psychoanalyst, the assembled company his patients, the hypnotic experience the cure. In this metaphorical therapy, the patients are cured of their dangerous urges by being forced to act out their fatal conclusions. The hypnotic trance takes on a didactic function: it reveals these hidden forces fully, and in so doing robs them of their power.

Yet Kracauer's language suggests a slippage between the medical and the magical: the illusionist is a "wizard" who uses "white magic" in the process of this "magical therapy." He is, then, much like those itinerant hypnotists who used the technique not to heal, but to fascinate. Indeed, we should recall that even ostensibly scientific demonstrations often contained an element of spectacle and performance. In *Warning Shadows*, though the depictions of infidelity and murder are framed as "only" the hallucinations of hypnotized characters, they are also staged as entertainment, intended to titillate. It is striking that the violence against the wife—the extended chase sequence, her increasing vulnerability, and finally her murder, staged in such a way as to suggest sexual violence—occupies so much of the episode. Cross-cutting between shots of her and those of the husband and guests builds tension and delays the viewer's experience of resolution and gratification. This speaks to the appeal of that violent submission as spectacle: the hallucination stages the sexual excess of a woman as well as her violent punishment for her transgression of patriarchal norms.

What Lies Beneath: Gender and Violence

The brutality of the wife's subjugation is something we risk losing sight of when we focus so strongly on the structure of the film: does the framing of her murder as a hallucination gives us leave to watch the scene in a less critical way? When we watch again the ostensible climax of the film, in which the woman is dragged back to face her angry husband, tied down on the table as though she were a sacrifice, then stabbed to death by the four men who previously did nothing but admire and desire her, it's difficult not to be struck by

Figure 27. Violence and gratification.

the violence of the scene. And this is a violence linked with erotic gratification, however sadistic: we see that on the face of the younger servant as the wife cowers next to him (0:51:27, fig. 27); certainly, the murder itself, in which we see the woman's shadow on the wall as she is stabbed (fig. 24), can be read as a metaphorical representation of sexual violence.

However much the film explains away the violence by revealing it—after the fact—as having been nothing but a hallucination, what remains undeniable is that we viewers watched the brutal spectacle unfold on screen as though it *were*, in the diegesis of the film, "real." Indeed, returning to the question that troubles so much early film, namely its revelation of the inability to distinguish between what is and is not real, perhaps it doesn't matter that the wife's death is

Figure 28. Cured or traumatized?

couched narratively as "unreal": that differentiation has little effect on the viewer's perception, save as a convenient way to excuse whatever satisfaction is derived from watching the scene.

And yet, there remains a discomfort even when the violence is explained away. The film itself models that discomfort: in the face of the wife, who, even after the hallucination has ended, appears not so much cured of her illegitimate desires as she seems traumatized, looking at her husband with obvious fear as he leans over her (1:16:50, fig. 28); in the demeanor of her admirers, who sheepishly depart. In a sense, that residual distress or shame points to the viewer's own implication in a scene that revels in staging a woman's abjection.

The spectacle of the wife's punishment, of course, is by no means unique in film. Even if we confine ourselves to German films from the Weimar era, we find a veritable catalogue of cinematic women who pay for their various transgressions in elaborately staged scenes. In Lubitsch's *Carmen* (1918), the eponymous heroine is stabbed to death for her promiscuity; in his *Madame Dubarry*, the titular woman again meets a fatal end when she is guillotined and her head thrown to the enthusiastic crowd for her crime of daring to rise from seamstress to king's mistress. In *Metropolis*, the lascivious robot Maria is burned at the stake in front of a crowd roaring for her death. And Pabst's *Büchse der Pandora* (*Pandora's Box*, 1929) punishes Lulu's sexual transgression with murder by none other than Jack the Ripper. Weimar cinema is littered with the corpses of women who dared transgress social norms.

And Weimar Germany was a time in which those norms were rapidly changing. The shift that saw women moving increasingly into employment outside the domestic sphere, begun out of necessity when they filled vital jobs during World War I, continued into the Weimar era. Politically, the Weimar constitution guaranteed women not just the vote, but broader equality. The style that came to embody Weimar modernity, the New Woman with her short skirts, bobbed hair, and masculine habits like smoking, was a visible manifestation of an emancipation often coded as physical. Given these social developments, the frequency with which films of the era forestall women's desire, agency, and independence is striking. In centering violence as a punishment for a woman's (perceived) transgression and constructing it as the catalyst for behavioral changes that restore balance, *Warning Shadows* reveals much about the anxieties bound up with women's roles at the time. If the hallucination does function as a sort of "therapy," as Kracauer would have it, then it is a process predicated not so much on revealing unconscious desires and urges as on removing a threat posed by a woman's unruly desire. That ostensible resolution sits uneasily with the discomfort of the wife and the couple's guests after the hallucinatory episode, suggesting that we should question whether the ending is as happy as it superficially appears. Doubly so given the closing moments of the film, when the guests have departed and the couple stands at the window overlooking the market outside: we see the illusionist jump onto a pig and ride it out of the square in an instance of such absurdity that one can't help but wonder whether it is meant to suggest that the happy ending is equally as absurd.

Just how questionable the "therapeutic" process in *Warning Shadows* is becomes more visible if we compare it to another film about unconscious urges, Pabst's *Secrets of a Soul*. *Secrets* focuses on a man who finds himself suddenly seized by a fear of knives and a compulsion to stab his wife (played, as previously noted, by the same Ruth Weyher who stars as the wife in *Warning Shadows*). As these urges become stronger, the husband seeks out psychoanalytical therapy, where he relates his dreams and visions to the sympathetic analyst and is ultimately cured. *Secrets* largely avoids reenacting the slippage between real and hallucination or dream that we see in *Warning Shadows*: it announces the troubled husband's nightmares by cutting between them and shots of his sleeping face, or by prefacing his account of his dream with an intertitle identifying it as such. The logic of these sequences, too, is markedly dreamlike, dispensing with the type of realism that we see in the hallucinatory episode in *Warning Shadows*. The viewer might be puzzled by the man's behavior or curious about the reasons for his action, but is surely not unable to identify the line between his hallucinations and the reality of the film. And, unlike in *Warning Shadows*, the fidelity of the wife in *Secrets* is never called into question: the husband's jealousy and rage is clearly unconnected to her actions, and the resolution of their relationship is due entirely to his cure, rather than to any change in her behavior.

A comparison between the two films might suggest that *Warning Shadows* is driven less by a desire to depict a cure for the irrational urges that dominate its characters than it is propelled by artistic ambition: it seems to purposely create and maintain in the viewer a sense of uncertainty, an inability to identify what is and what isn't real. That it does so via a central spectacle of female abjection is in one sense secondary to that effect and in another crucial, as it begs the question of how much films like *Warning Shadows* set a precedent or take part in shaping the development of filmic norms that, for a long time, relegated female characters to passive positions as objects of desire, staged for a viewer aligned with a patriarchal gaze.[109]

The Hypnotic Screen

The shadows and reflections at the heart of Robison's film, as discussed previously, connect to the ways in which film itself has been conceptualized; hypnotism, too, is linked to the ways that cinema has been theorized. As early as 1916, German-born psychologist Hugo Münsterberg discussed the way that film works on the mind in terms that draw parallels to hypnotism. Considering how the mind responds to the images of a film, he argues that film holds more power over perceptions than does, for example, theater. Both use "suggestion" to spur in the viewer associations that are "completely controlled by our own interest and attitude and by our previous experiences."[110] Film, however, can limit the subjectivity of associations and manipulate the viewer. It can, for example, cut from one scene to another without leaving the viewer time to form a complete chain of associations and thereby "complete" the truncated action; as Münsterberg states, "there is no need of bringing the series of pictures to its logical end, because they are pictures only and not the real objects."[111] Münsterberg explicitly links the power of such suggestion that film exerts to hypnosis: "The extreme case is, of course, that of the hypnotizer whose word awakens in the mind of the hypnotized person ideas which he cannot resist. He must accept them as real, he must believe that the dreary room is a beautiful garden in which he picks flowers. The spellbound audience in a theater or in a picture house is certainly in a state of heightened suggestibility and is ready to receive suggestions."[112]

Münsterberg's linkage between cinema and hypnotism was by no means unique. Some framed this connection negatively, conflating the anxiety about hypnotism and its potentially deleterious effects with the fears regarding cinema that motivated both the *Kinoreform* movement and censorship. Andreas Killen points to the fact that film developed just at the time when mass psychology was being theorized, and that hypnosis was figured as a key term in that conceptualization: "In the writings of Gustave Le Bon, Gabriel Tarde, and others, it seemed to capture a frightening otherness at the heart of modern society: a kind of collective action that could take uncanny and violent forms."[113] Killen notes that the concept of "suggestion" was central to the anxious discourses focused on the masses, on film, and on hypnotism.[114] Little wonder, then, that these anxieties become bound up with one another: the mass medium of cinema functions as another form of hypnotism, itself an object of mass fascination and, simultaneously, a tool of potential manipulation.

The peculiar affinity between film and states like hypnosis, hallucination, and dream has drawn interest since the beginning of the medium and well into contemporary thought.[115] That cinema continues to be theorized in terms of hypnosis and suggestion explains in some ways its peculiar status, especially in the early twentieth century: simultaneously lauded as a potential force for public enlightenment and feared as a means of control over the masses, film's fascinating power occupied as ambivalent a position as hypnosis did in *Warning Shadows*'s cultural context. Killen notes that the spectator of hypnotic exhibition should not be construed as entirely passive: rather, because performers often unveiled some of the mechanisms behind their performances, "Weimar audience members who attended such performances are perhaps better seen as participants in a complex public ceremony that negotiated the unstable boundary between science and magic. ... The result was a complicated orchestration of spectatorial engagement and disenchantment."[116] The performance of hypnosis thus could serve not only to exert power over the spectators, but also to return some measure of it to them through the revelation of the mechanisms at the root of hypnotic control. With this in mind, we should ask ourselves whether *Warning Shadows* engages in a similar process of "disenchantment," staging its own illusions in such a way as to reveal their secrets and, in doing so, not only entrancing the viewers, but also enlightening them.

The Other Projection: The Chinese Shadow Play

The hallucinatory episode at the center of *Warning Shadows* tends to draw all of our attention, eclipsing the performance that it interrupts: the Chinese shadow play that the illusionist stages for the couple and their guests. In a film that reflects on the cinematic medium in so many ways, however, the depiction of the shadow play is not merely a footnote, but deserves closer consideration. It begins much as a film screening would: The lights in the room have been dimmed. We see a medium shot of the illusionist as he crouches down next to a chair positioned at the end of the table, sets a bottle with a lit candle in it on the seat and positions it carefully as he looks at the canvas that has been hung on the wall, then glances towards the couple and their guests off-screen. As he prepares for the shadow play, he makes a peculiar gesture, clenching his hands next to his face and then opening them as though throwing something onto the screen, pursing his lips as though he's blowing at it (0:30:55, fig. 29). He does this once, twice, much as a magician would accompany a trick with a physical flourish. We cut to a medium shot of the audience seated in a row. The wife's eyes seem closed; the youth is distracted; though not yet hypnotized, they appear only half-conscious. Then a long shot of the room with the illusionist on the right, casting his

Figure 29. Projecting magic.

first shadow for the assembled spectators. The shadow of a dragon slowly crosses the canvas, but the show is interrupted with a cut to the woman and the youth, as his hand slowly moves towards hers. In a close-up, the wife moves her hand further onto her lap, then the sequence cuts to a medium shot of the visibly angry husband leaning against the wall, before returning to the illusionist as he picks up a mysterious piece of paper. The sequence returns to a long shot of the room, showing a shadow frame slowly slide onto the canvas, then to a long shot of the screen from a slightly different angle, positioning us almost directly behind the viewers at the table and hiding the illusionist from us.

The shadow play begins and two women appear on the screen: one holds a mirror for the other, then leaves, and a man joins the remaining woman, bringing her a flower that she admires before they kiss. Twice the maid comes in—twice the woman gestures her away. On her third entrance, she and her mistress pull the man off-screen. The woman returns and a second man enters, this one stockier: he seems to embody brutality. She kisses him, then fetches a ball of yarn. He raises his hands and she begins to wrap the yarn around them. Here, the play is again interrupted briefly, as the sequence cuts to a long shot of the table, as the youth, laughing, turns towards the woman seated next to him. Returning to the screen, we see the second man as he falls asleep, his hands now literally tied; the woman gestures and is joined on screen by the man she has hidden. Several times, he approaches her, then draws back. Another interruption: the sequence cuts to a reaction shot of two of the wife's admirers: they turn slowly to each other and one winks (0:33:59). Back in the shadow play, the woman finally approaches the man and kisses him (0:34:16, fig. 30).

But the story is interrupted yet again, by a medium shot of the illusionist as he pauses and looks towards his audience, then a close-up showing the youth's hand and that of the wife, dangerously close. As noted above, the interruption shows how misleading shadows are: as the husband watches, the hands move closer, while the illusionist shifts his candle to create a close-up of the hands' shadows (fig. 14): the shadows are touching, as though the hands are clasped. The husband's angry investigation finds nothing, and the assembled spectators laugh. We cut back to the illusionist, but not to return to the silhouette play, at least not yet (0:35:43): this is the moment just before he hypnotizes his viewers. Soon enough, they will become the shadows on the screen.

Far from being merely the frame for the hallucinatory episode, the shadow play is significant in multiple ways. In the context of the early 1920s, it is an example of an art form that was a popular part of public entertainment, whether in advertisements, short films, or features. Within *Warning Shadows*, it is one of the multiple forms of shadows that we see, rehearsing, in a sense, the events of the hypnotic

Figure 30. On-screen infidelity, foreshadowing what is to come.

episode. Considered more broadly, in light of the multiple ways in which *Warning Shadows* reflects on the medium itself, the shadow play, like shadowgraphy and magic lantern projections, is also a forerunner of film. As one of the many iterations of shadow play in the film, it complicates its structure and reminds us of the film as film, contributing to the way that *Warning Shadows*, like the public performances of hypnosis, oscillates between illusion and revelation.

The *Schattentheater*, shadow or silhouette play, was not new in the 1920s; as Heide Schönemann notes, the art form, rooted in Chinese shadow plays, had been periodically in vogue since the eighteenth century.[117] Its return to popularity in the late nineteenth and early twentieth centuries coincides with the invention and dissemination of cinema, but seems more broadly linked to modernity. Nancy

Forgione suggests that a similar interest in shadows in France in the late nineteenth century was connected to the increasing awareness and investigation of the human psyche; the shadow served to stand in for "the truth behind appearances," to represent "the less apparent underside, inside, or dark side of people and things"[118]—precisely those areas under investigation in psychoanalysis (and equally central to hypnotism). In its traditional form, the shadow play would have worked by moving silhouettes behind a screen with a light source positioned to cast their shadows, while the audience sat on the other side.[119] With the development of cinema, however, we see the traditional form adapt to the new technology. Certainly, not everyone saw an affinity in the forms; in 1907, Georg Jacob denied any relationship between the shadow play and cinema, claiming that any connection is superficial and that "the shadow stage is vastly superior to the cinema, not because it can give its objects color and language in addition to movement, but rather because it is no mere mirror of reality."[120] And yet, the shadow play has both literal and metaphorical parallels to live-action film, where the figures on screen are equally "shadows," however real they may seem.

Indeed, just twelve years after Jacob scoffed at the comparison of film to the shadow play, the most famous of silhouette filmmakers, Lotte Reiniger, released her first short, *Das Ornament des verliebten Herzens* (*The Ornament of the Lovestruck Heart*, 1919). Trained as an actor with Max Reinhardt, Reiniger's talent for cutting silhouettes had gained her the notice of Paul Wegener, who not only included her work in several of his films, but also opened doors for her at the Institut für Kulturforschung (Institute of Cultural Research), which would produce many of her early works.[121] Reiniger made short films, many based on fairy tales, as well as advertisements. Perhaps surprisingly, Robison did not enlist Reiniger for the shadow play in *Warning Shadows*, working instead with Ernst Moritz Engert, an artist who is, at least now, less well known.[122] Still, we find distinct parallels between the aesthetics of Engert's shadow play in *Warning*

Shadows and Reiniger's work. It may well be that Reiniger was too busy when Robison was filming in 1923: that year, she started work on her first full-length silhouette film, *The Adventures of Prince Achmed*, a piece that would take several years of painstaking work before its release. While Reiniger's work is known, it has not been given a great deal of scholarly attention[123]—similar in this way to *Warning Shadows*. And indeed, in the centering of the artistic process that we find in both Reiniger's films and in *Warning Shadows*, we can find another parallel. This did not go unremarked: in 1929, an article on the avant-garde film, which the author defined as "tomorrow's film, as it is already seen today by the eyes of artists working abstractly," counted both *Warning Shadows* and Reiniger's *Prince Achmed* among the group.[124]

Thematically, the shadow play in *Warning Shadows* integrates seamlessly into Robison's narrative as one of the multiple ways in which the central conflict in the film is portrayed. At the outset, the shadow play sets up the tension that we see in the triangulation of the couple and the youth: the shadow play, too, introduces a wife engaged in an illicit affair and an enraged husband. The play is interrupted just at the moment in which the wife and her lover kiss; instead of seeing the denouement of her actions, we first witness the violent punishment of the flesh-and-blood wife—or at least of her shadow double—in the hypnotic episode. When we, along with the characters, are released from the spell, we find ourselves right where the shadow play left off. The illusionist offers to continue (1:13:37); while the guests demur, the husband overrules them. With the audience back in their original seats, the screen again framed in a long shot with the camera located behind them, the play continues: the shadow husband awakens to see his wife with her lover, shakes off the wool that binds his hands, raises his sword, and brutally slices his rival straight down the middle (1:14:25, fig. 31). As before, we cut away to reaction shots of the guests and the wife: this time, they are spellbound by the shadows in front of them.

Figure 31. Punishing a rival.

Back on the screen, the shadow wife enters, offers the sword to her husband, and bows as though expecting execution. Instead, he drops the weapon and they kiss, then he goes to his rival and, with a flick of his wrist, reassembles his body. As the couple continues to embrace, the lover approaches them, but is gestured away by the wife. The couple leaves the frame, the maid follows them across the stage one last time, and then the shadow play ends. We cut back to the illusionist, who folds up the cutout frame as he rises, then to a shot of the table, with the youth, the woman, and one of the guests sitting as though shell-shocked; only the husband shows much enthusiasm, rising and applauding (1:16:20).

The shadow play presents a vision of the conflict in *Warning Shadows* altered only so much as to shift the deadly punishment

Figure 32. Cuckold or devil?

from wife to lover. And in the play, too, death is not permanent, but is reversed once the wife has repented—just as the wife's murder in the hypnotic experience is undone once they awaken. At the same time, the shadow play is only one of many re-inscriptions of that conflict in the film, which stages the wife's vanity, dominance, and desire, as well as the husband's weakness, jealousy, and violence, again and again: through the shadow play and the hypnotic episode, but also in the brief moment when the illusionist first demonstrates his skills to the servants by casting the shadow of a couple kissing passionately, or when the husband stands in the study and realizes that his shadow has aligned with a set of antlers on the wall, making him appear as cuckold—or devil (0:51:57, fig. 32). There are the shadows cast by the wife—her body on the door as shadows appear to caress her, or her hand as the youth seems to grasp it: shadows that suggest one reality, but are actually the results of a very different one. In its artifice, the shadow play reminds the viewer that the rest of the film, too, is not reality, but merely appearance: manipulated, easily misunderstood, ambiguous.

In this way, the shadow play points back to *Warning Shadows* as a whole, reflecting on the film as representative of the medium itself. The multiplication of the conflict that is ostensibly at the heart of the film draws attention to its ambiguity and reminds us of its own shadowy status: however real the events might look, however much we might think that we understand them, they are, in the end, never what they appear. Christian Metz argues that film is fundamentally characterized by a gap between its apparent reality and its actual status, noting that cinema's "perceptions are all in a sense 'false'. Or rather, the activity of perception which it involves is real (the cinema is not a phantasy), but the perceived is not really the object, it is its shade, its phantom, its double, its *replica* in a new kind of mirror."[125] Metz's analysis speaks to the very structure of film: even as it appears to represent the real—recall Jacob's derisive notion of it as a mere "mirror of reality"[126]—it is precisely *not* this; rather, it is structured by an organizing falseness, by the notion that what is *perceived* is what is real. We should think about *Warning Shadows* in light of this: it, too, reminds us of the gap between appearance and real, not only in terms of our interpretation of events and feelings, but also in terms of simple mis-seeings, mis-readings, mis-takings of a shot, a scene, a sequence. Everything that we think we know about *Warning Shadows* is challenged and undermined over the course of the film. Is the wife adulterous, or merely flirtatious and vain? Are the sideways glances, the winks, the body language indicative of what is actually occurring in whatever reality the film has? Or are they all representations of a specific perspective? If so, whose? Is what we witness determined by the jealousy and rage that shape the husband's perception of the events? Or is there a neutral perspective that we are shown?

Thinking about *Warning Shadows* as a film that centers its filmic quality in this way also pushes us to reflect on what the portrayal of the illusionist says about Robison's self-consciousness as filmmaker. As discussed, the illusionist, who guides the viewer through the narrative even while he arranges and participates it in, takes on multiple roles. He is associated with hypnotism as both medical therapy and public entertainment and with magic performances, shadowgraphy, and shadow play; at the same time, he breaks the boundary between the film and its audience by acknowledging the camera from the start. In a very real sense, the illusionist thus becomes an overdetermined figure. If this is Robison's vision of his position as filmmaker, then it speaks to his estimation of the potential of cinema as art form, as mass entertainment, and yet equally so as means of public enlightenment. Robison himself, in reflecting on the role of the director and the process of making a film, suggested that the task of acting was one that should not be left to the actors, who should be chosen to fit the roles they are to inhabit based on type rather than on skill; instead, he noted, "the only one who must act in a film is the director."[127] This suggestion lines up neatly with the position of the illusionist, reminding the viewer outside of the film that there is a key role that often goes unremarked, since the "presence" of the director is usually not so clearly marked in the diegesis. Here, the entertainer is a stand-in for Robison, and we are made privy to at least some of his tricks: shifting between shots aligned with those of the on-screen audience—when we are positioned behind them as we watch the silhouette play, or when we see, with no mediation or clear demarcation of its status as fantasy, the events of the hypnotic episode unreel—and shots in which we see more—when we are shown the same events from multiple perspectives so that the misunderstandings and illusions are revealed, or when we see explicitly the tools of the illusion, such as the shadow puppet that the illusionist holds and makes move one more time after the play is complete (1:18:00, fig. 33). As our spectatorial position vacillates, we

Figure 33. Tools of the trade.

are alternately spellbound and disenchanted, forcing us to reflect on the medium itself.

Conclusion: A More Complex History

What I find most remarkable about *Warning Shadows* is how complex and varied its cultural significance is: it engages with so many anxieties, preoccupations, and fascinations that characterized the cultural background at the time of its release, has connections to so many of the films and filmmakers that were central to German film history, and resonates with so many larger questions—focused not just on film, but also on the human psyche and perception broadly—that remain relevant today. In a sense, it—like the illusionist himself—seems overdetermined: to investigate the film leads not so much to a coherent understanding as it does to the revelation of yet another twist, yet another point that merits more analysis. In this, *Warning Shadows* exemplifies the potential value of films as objects of cultural study: it gives the audience a glimpse into its historical context and into the experiences of those other audiences for whom this film expressed, in some way, the content of their lives. As an article stated in 1919, "film is the mirror of its time":[128] beyond all of the projections, reflections, and shadows we see within *Warning Shadows*, it also reflects something larger than its own narrative, giving us a window onto the tumultuous moment that marked its premiere in October 1923. And even beyond its richness as a source for cultural and historical investigations, *Warning Shadows* raises questions that feel surprisingly current: about the dual function of film as capitalist product and as artistic medium, about the role of the unconscious in human behavior, about desire and gender and violence.

One peculiarity about the study of early German film is that it forces us to grapple with the knowledge that our understanding will never be complete, not just because of the difficulty of fully grasping the past from our own cultural and historical perspective, but also because, concretely, we will never have full access to the cinematic output of the era. The film industry of the Weimar Republic made more than 3,500 movies;[129] nowhere near that number has survived. As Anton Kaes explains, the business of film didn't aim at archiving and preserving. When the single-reel movies of early cinema gave way to longer, more narratively complex feature films, no one thought to memorialize what had been outgrown; rather, it was the raw stuff of film that was seen as more valuable than the images that stuff held: the silver and celluloid that could be recuperated by melting down the reels, or the money to be made by selling off individual parts of film reels as souvenirs.[130] What we're left with, then, is but a fraction of the movies that populated the screens of Weimar

Germany. Thousands of screens, because cinema was big business: by 1925 there were about 3,900 theaters, by 1930 more than 5,000.[131] Those theaters drew crowds. Indeed, cinema became an institution with the potential to transcend nations, cultures, and borders. In 1925, Richard Muckermann, journalist and later politician, waxed poetic about film's appeal and reach: "The asphalt shimmers—the damp evening fog is torn by sudden beams of light—dark crowds— the people—push and shove themselves across the street—not to a play, an art gallery, a recreation, a pleasure—but to the movies. And this pushing and shoving is not bound to time and place, it is something communal on this earth, almost more communal than humans themselves."[132] Muckermann articulates just how significant film was: for the masses throughout the world, film became the prime source of cultural experience.

The films that have survived for us to consider represent only a small part of what those viewers saw; the ones that have become what we might too blithely term "canonical" make up an even more narrow part. Peruse the pages of a film journal from the era and you'll come across so many tantalizing reviews from which you can just barely piece together a sense of what a movie might have been, and even more titles with nothing beyond production company and perhaps stars' names appended. And yet, to do justice to those masses who sought out the "communal" experience of film, to truly grasp the ways in which film reflected their anxieties, fantasies, and preoccupations, we need to think as expansively as possible about those artifacts that we do have access to, and to embed them as thoroughly as possible in their discursive context.

Warning Shadows is one of the fraction of films that has survived, and yet has been, in many ways, relegated to a footnote. Perhaps we follow the lead of the viewing public at the time in thus neglecting it. Kracauer noted that, "even though it belongs among the masterpieces of the German screen, *Warning Shadows* passed almost unnoticed," and quoted Fritz Arno Wagner, the cameraman, as saying that "'it only found response from the film aesthetes, making no impression on the general public.'"[133] If this is so, perhaps it was too ambitious, too artistic; perhaps the almost allegorical nature of the narration did not serve the kind of entertainment value that audiences sought out. Perhaps it was simply released in the wrong place and at the wrong time. *Warning Shadows* premiered in Berlin on October 16; that day, the local *Vossische Zeitung* reported on clashes between unemployed demonstrators and police.[134] Newspapers discussed the coming currency reform that would introduce the *Rentenmark*, the new currency, backed by the value of property instead of gold, that would stabilize the crippling inflation gripping Germany. But the introduction of the new currency and the resulting stabilization was still several weeks away. On the day that *Warning Shadows* premiered, a dollar was worth 4.1 billion Marks.[135] And *Warning Shadows* was competing with the likes of Joe May's *Tragödie der Liebe* (*The Tragedy of Love*), a multi-part crowd pleaser that premiered on October 8 and was billed "a sensational success on the part of May,"[136] and Hans Steinhoff's *Inge Larsen*, which opened at the *Kammer-Lichtspiele* on the same day as *Warning Shadows* and would be reviewed by the *Kinematograph* as "a film that will surely bring in big business for weeks."[137] In an environment fraught with existential deprivation, would films like these, playing more directly to audience expectations and interests, simply have held more appeal than Robison's artistically ambitious one?

It's tempting to explain the marginal position *Warning Shadows* occupies in what is today framed as the canon of German film as a result of its equally marginal position in its time. Yet doing so, blaming the film's neglect on a purported lack of success upon its release, is already adhering to a certain narrative about German film history. Was the film really so unnoticed in its time? Notwithstanding the evidence from Kracauer—who was writing twenty years after the release of *Warning Shadows*—we can equally find responses acknowledging the film's significance, as well as its popularity. In a November issue of the Viennese trade journal *Der Film-Bote*, Walter Thielemann reports from Berlin that "*Warning Shadows* has been running for three weeks with great success, certainly a notable achievement. In contrast, the Henny Porten film *Inge Larsen* wasn't able to keep its place on the movie schedule for long. Shouldn't that be a strong sign that the audience wants to see new faces in film?"[138] Thielemann's comment pushes us to reevaluate the way that we position films like *Warning Shadows*: taking into account those same "new faces" that appealed to the audiences in 1923 might help us to generate the kind of nuanced and varied understanding of the era's cultural and cinematic production that we should strive for. The same ambition that at times makes *Warning Shadows* seem overly complicated or inconsistent is what makes it such a valuable object of study. There are films that can be more easily interpreted in a coherent way, or that might not seem quite so visually and aesthetically strange as *Warning Shadows*, where the stylized opening, echoed by intermittent shots of curtains falling in order to indicate the ends of a scene, contrasts so sharply with sequences that are shot in an essentially realist way. But *Warning Shadows* is a film that is so dense with significance that *not* considering it as part of the broader landscape of Weimar cinema means losing key insights, not only into the multiple cultural discourses and preoccupations that the film thematizes, but also into the potential of film to function in such a rich way.

In his 1923 analysis of *Warning Shadows*, Paul Hildebrandt argued that the ending serves to disperse "the unreal, the abstract, the imaginary," that the peculiar moment in which the illusionist rides off on a pig is a "Shakespearean gesture" that serves as his statement that "'la comedia é finita.'"[139] But the strength of *Warning Shadows* seems to lie precisely in the sense that the end of the film does not, as Hildebrandt would have it, disperse the strangeness of the tale and leave the audience breathing easily: rather, it nags at us, bothers us, strikes us simultaneously as terribly unfamiliar and as hauntingly modern. As counterintuitive as it might sound, *Warning Shadows* reads as "current" in a way that few films of the era do: however unfamiliar the aesthetics of the film might seem to contemporary audiences, there is a daring quality to the film that might surprise a viewer today, but actually serves as a reminder that modernity has its roots long in the past. This is what makes *Warning Shadows* so compelling: it becomes both a nexus for the anxieties and desires that motivated audiences in 1923 and a window onto the ways in which we can trace so many of our own fears and preoccupations into the past.

CREDITS

Director:
Artur Robison

Idea:
Albin Grau

Writers:
Rudolf Schneider
Artur Robison

Cinematography:
Fritz Arno Wagner

Art Direction:
Albin Grau

Costume Design:
Albin Grau

Music (at the premiere in Berlin):
Ernst Riege

Cast:
Fritz Kortner (Husband)
Ruth Weyher (Wife)
Gustav von Wangenheim (Youth)
Alexander Granach (Illusionist)
Eugen Rex (Admirer)
Max Gülstorff (Admirer)
Ferdinand von Alten (Admirer)
Fritz Rasp (Young Servant)
Karl Platen (Older Servant)
Lilly Harder (Maid)

Production Company:
Pan-Film GmbH (Berlin)
Deutsch-Amerikanische Film-Union AG
    (Dafu) (Berlin)

Producers:
Enrico Dieckmann
Willy Seibold

Executive Producer:
Enrico Dieckmann

Distribution:
Deutsch-Amerikanische Film-Union AG
    (Dafu) (Berlin)

Sound:
silent

Color:
b/w, tinted

Aspect Ratio:
1.33:1

Film Length:
2002 m (original version without
    intertitles submitted to censor
    board)
2036 m (version with intertitles submitted
    to board simultaneously)
85 min. (restored ZDF/ARTE/absolut
    Medien DVD version)

Negative Format:
35 mm

Cinematographic Process:
Spherical

Release Dates:
October 1923 (Germany), September
    1924 (France)

NOTES

1   This was one of several such subtitles, as I will discuss later.

2   James C. Franklin, "Metamorphosis of a Metaphor: The Shadow in Early German Cinema," *German Quarterly* 53, no. 2 (March 1980): 182.

3   Unsigned review of *Schatten*, *Film-Kurier*, July 27, 1923. Unless otherwise noted, all translations are my own.

4   Sabine Hake, "Expressionism and Cinema: Reflections on a Phantasmagoria of Film History," in *A Companion to the Literature of German Expressionism*, ed. Neil H. Donahue (Rochester, NY: Camden House, 2005), 331.

5   S. S. Prawer, *Caligari's Children: The Film as Tale of Terror* (Oxford: Oxford University Press, 1980), 32.

6   Anton Kaes, "German Cultural History and the Study of Film: Ten Theses and a Postscript," *New German Critique* 65 (Spring/Summer 1995): 51.

7   Screenshots from and time stamps for *Warning Shadows* are taken from the restored version released on DVD in the ARTE Edition/absolut Medien series in 2016.

8   Screenshot is taken from the restored version produced by the Friedrich-Wilhelm-Murnau-Stiftung, ZDF, and ARTE and released on DVD by Transit Film in 2014.

9   E. B., "Filmschau," review of *Schatten*, *Vorwärts*, July 29, 1923, 9.

10 Artur Robison in *Filmkünstler: Wir über uns selbst*, ed. Hermann Treuner (Berlin: Sibyllen-Verlag, 1928), n. p.

11 Robison wrote and directed *Des Nächsten Weib* (*Thy Neighbor's Wife*, with Franz Seitz Sr.) and *Nächte des Grauens* (*Nights of Horror*, 1917), in addition to writing *Die Frau mit den zwei Seelen* (*The Woman with Two Souls*, Heinrich von Korff, 1916), all three starring Synd and all presumably lost.

12 Filmportal.de lists an earlier film, *Der Schmuck der Herzogin* (*The Duchess's Jewels*, Siegfried Philippi, 1916) as a Pan-Film-GmbH production; however, the date is early, and based on advertising for *Schmuck*, it seems that this was in fact a Sascha-Messterfilm production. "Advertisement for *Der Schmuck der Herzogin*," *Neue Kino-Rundschau*, December 15, 1917, 11.

13 Anton Kaes, "Schatten: Eine nächtliche Halluzination," 2017, http://www.giornatedel cinemamuto.it/anno/2017/en/schatten-eine-nachtliche-halluzination/index.html.

14 F. P., review of *Zwischen Abend und Morgen*, *Die Filmwelt* 10 (1923): 5.

15 E. B., "Filmschau," 7.

16 "Unter der Lupe," *Kinematographische Monatshefte* 7 (July 1923): 8.

17 These articles are presented as autobiographical, though it's unclear whether they were in fact written by Weyher or were simply framed as such to appeal to the reader. Pictured: Ruth Weyher, "Mein Leben," *Ufa-Magazin*, April 1–7, 1927. See also: Ruth Weyher, "Wir drehen in Paris," *Ufa-Magazin*, March 25–31, 1927; Ruth Weyher, "Der Tag einer Diva," *Mein Film* 78 (1927): 3; Ruth Weyher, ". . . denn in der Wanne schwimmt ein riesengrosser Schwamm!," *Mein Film* 119 (1928): 4–5.

18 Weyher was cast in *Sei gegrüßt, Du mein schönes Sorrent* (*Greetings, beautiful Sorrento*), alternately titled *Der Mann für eine Nacht* (*The Man for One Night*, Romano Mengon, 1930), and in a minor role in *Das Geheimnis der fünf Schlüssel/Im Kampf mit der Unterwelt* (*The Secret of the Five Keys/Battle with the Underworld*, Carlo Aldini, 1930); neither film seems to have been especially successful. After those roles, she is mentioned in the press only peripherally: for example, in an issue of *Mein Film*, editors respond to a reader's query by noting that they haven't heard any news regarding Weyher ("Meine Filmpost," *Mein Film* 338 [1932]: 16). While some sources suggest that she married in 1932, newspapers report that, in November of 1933, she was in fact living under her maiden name in Berlin with her brother (from articles reporting a robbery in her home; *Berliner Morgenpost*, November 14, 1933, 6).

19 "Die Eröffnung des Cines-Nollendorf-Theaters in Berlin," *Der Kinematograph*, March 26, 1913.

20 Siegfried Kracauer, "Cult of Distraction: On Berlin's Picture Palaces," trans. Thomas Y. Levin, *New German Critique* 40 (Winter 1987): 91.

21 "Die Eröffnung des Cines-Nollendorf-Theaters in Berlin."

22 While *Metropolis's* initial gala premiere took place at the Ufa-Palast am Zoo, Janet Ward notes that there was another premiere at the Ufa-Pavilion Nollendorfplatz, as the Union Theater was by then called. Janet Ward, *Weimar Surfaces: Urban Visual Culture in 1920s Germany* (Berkeley: University of California Press, 2001), 166–67. After the initial opening, *Metropolis* was then screened only at the Nollendorfplatz theater. Thomas Elsaesser, *Metropolis*, BFI Film Classics (London: British Film Institute, 2000), 29–30.

23 Unsigned review of *Schatten*, *Film-Kurier*, October 17, 1923, 1.

24 Unsigned review of *Schatten*, *Der Film-Bote*, January 12, 1924, 17.

25 Paul Hildebrandt, "Schatten: Eine Analyse," *Kinematographische Monatshefte* 10–11 (October/November 1923): 1.

26 "Unter der Lupe," 8.

27 Advertisement for *Schatten*, *Der Kinematograph*, October 14, 1923.

28 Sabine Hake, *The Cinema's Third Machine: Writing on Film in Germany 1907–1933* (Lincoln/London: University of Nebraska Press, 1993), xii.

29 Joseph Garncarz, "The Origins of Film Exhibition in Germany," in *The German Cinema Book*, ed. Tim Bergfelder, Erica Carter, and Deniz Göztürk (London: British Film Institute, 2002), 115.

30 Garncarz, "The Origins of Film Exhibition in Germany," 115.

31   Garncarz notes that the admission prices for the *Ladenkinos*, lower than those of the traveling shows or the variety theaters, indicate this; in addition, he cites Emilie Altenloh's *Zur Soziologie des Kinos* (On the Sociology of Cinema), which draws on the example of movie audiences in Mannheim to show that they were made up of "mainly blue-collar and lower-status white-collar workers." Quotations in text and note are from Garncarz, "The Origins of Film Exhibition in Germany," 117.

32   Scott Curtis, "The Taste of a Nation: Training the Senses and Sensibility of Cinema Audiences in Imperial Germany," *Film History* 6, no. 4 (1994): 448.

33   Curtis, "The Taste of a Nation," 450.

34   Curtis, "The Taste of a Nation," 452.

35   Curtis, "The Taste of a Nation," 453.

36   Hake, *The Cinema's Third Machine*, 50.

37   Hermann Häfker, *Kino und Kunst* (Mönchen Gladbach: Lichtbilderei Volksverein-Verlag, 1913), 8, https://www.gutenberg.org/files/45725/45725-h/45725-h.htm, Project Gutenberg EBook (2014).

38   Häfker, *Kino und Kunst*, 14.

39   Häfker, *Kino und Kunst*, 45–46.

40   Häfker, *Kino und Kunst*, 47.

41   "Wechselbalg." Häfker, *Kino und Kunst*, 42.

42   Ward, *Weimar Surfaces*, 163.

43   Thomas Elsaesser, *Weimar Cinema and After: Germany's Historical Imaginary* (London and New York: Routledge, 2000), 39.

44   Erich Staude, "Der Kampf um den Zwischentitel. Beitrag zur Filmdramaturgie," *Kinematographische Monatshefte* 5 (May 1923): 8.

45   Staude, "Der Kampf um den Zwischentitel," 9.

46   It seems likely that this is the same Walter Jonas who wrote a number of screenplays between 1925 and 1931; in two of these, incidentally, Ruth Weyher was cast.

47   All quotations in this section are from Walter Jonas, "Warum keine Titel," *Film-Kurier*, January 14, 1924. Carl Mayer wrote the screenplay not only for *New Year's Eve*, but indeed for all of the films without intertitles here mentioned excepting *Warning Shadows*.

48   Artur Robison, "Warum kein titelloser Film? Eine Erwiderung," *Beiblatt zum Film-Kurier*, January 19, 1924.

49   Robison, "Warum kein titelloser Film."

50   Robison refers to a souvenir cast of the title figure of Josef Victor von Scheffel's poem *The Trumpeter of Säckingen*, presumably as an epitome of kitsch. Robison, "Warum kein titelloser Film."

51   Robison, "Warum kein titelloser Film."

52   Robison, "Warum kein titelloser Film."

53   Ufa was initially founded in 1917 by consolidating a number of influential produc-
     tion companies, Messter-Film, Nordische Film GmbH, and Projektions-AG Union
     (PAGU), and quickly grew, absorbing many of the other smaller companies. In the
     mid-1920s, Ufa flourished, producing everything from weekly newsreels to popular en-
     tertainment movies to such classics as *Metropolis* and *The Blue Angel*. During the Third
     Reich, it was essentially nationalized and again enjoyed enormous success. After 1945,
     its influence waned, though it survives in some form, having been purchased in 1964 by
     the media company Bertelsmann.

54   Robison in Treuner, ed., *Filmkünstler: Wir über uns selbst.*

55   Unsigned review of *Schatten, Film-Kurier,* July 27, 1923.

56   Unsigned review of *Schatten, Der Film-Bote,* February 2, 1924, 12.

57   Unsigned review of *Schatten, Der Film-Bote,* January 12, 1924, 17.

58   Lotte Eisner, *The Haunted Screen: Expressionism in the German Cinema and the Influence
     of Max Reinhardt,* trans. Roger Greaves (Berkeley: University of California Press, 1973),
     137.

59   Gerhard Lamprecht, *Deutsche Stummfilme,* 10 vols., vol. 8: *1923–1926* (Berlin: Deutsche
     Kinemathek, 1967), 172–73.

60   James D. Steakley, "Cinema and Censorship in the Weimar Republic: The Case of
     Anders als die Andern," *Film History* 11, no. 2 (1999): 190.

61   Jeanpaul Goergen, "Der pikante Film. Ein vergessenes Genre der Kaiserzeit," in *Kino
     der Kaiserzeit: Zwischen Tradition und Moderne,* ed. Thomas Elsaesser and Michael
     Wedel (Munich: edition text + kritik, 2002), 45.

62   Kai Nowak, *Projektionen der Moral: Filmskandale in der Weimarer Republik* (Göttingen:
     Wallstein Verlag, 2015), 144–45.

63   Gary D. Stark, "Aroused Authorities: State Efforts to Regulate Sex and Smut in the
     German Mass Media, 1880–1930," in *Not Straight from Germany: Sexual Publics and
     Sexual Citizenship since Magnus Hirschfeld,* ed. Michael Thomas Taylor, Annette F.
     Timm, and Rainer Herrn (Ann Arbor: University of Michigan Press, 2017), 114.

64   Erika Hughes, "Art and illegality on the Weimar stage. The dances of Celly de Rheydt,
     Anita Berber and Valeska Gert," *Journal of European Studies* 39, no. 3 (2009): 326–27.

65   Susan Laikin Funkenstein, "Anita Berber: Imaging a Weimar Performance Artist,"
     Woman's Art Journal 26, no. 1 (Spring/Summer 2005): 27.

66   "Theater und Kunst," *Illustrierte Kronen-Zeitung* (Vienna), May 8, 1923, 7.

67   E. H. Gombrich, *Shadows: The Depiction of Cast Shadows in Western Art* (New Haven,
     CT: Yale University Press, 2014), unpaginated.

68   Gorky's piece was originally published in 1896. Maxim Gorky, "A review of the Lumière
     programme," trans. Leda Swan, in *Kino: A History of the Russian and Soviet Film,* ed. Jay
     Leyda (London: George Allan & Unwin, 1960), 407.

69   Victor I. Stoichita, *A Short History of the Shadow*, trans. Anne-Marie Glasheen (London: Reaktion Books, 1997), 150, 152.

70   Anton Kaes, *Shell Shock Cinema: Weimar Culture and the Wounds of War* (Princeton, NJ: Princeton University Press, 2009), 126.

71   Katharina Loew, *Special Effects and German Silent Film: Techno-Romantic Cinema* (Amsterdam: Amsterdam University Press, 2021), 114.

72   Erik Barnouw, *The Magician and the Cinema* (New York and Oxford: Oxford University Press, 1981), 16.

73   Barnouw, *The Magician and the Cinema*, 87.

74   Barnouw, *The Magician and the Cinema*, 87–88.

75   Barnouw, *The Magician and the Cinema*, 9.

76   John Grand-Carteret, "La silhouette sous ses formes diverses," *Revue encyclopédique: recueil documentaire universel et illustré* 2 (1892): 1722.

77   Barnouw, *The Magician and the Cinema*, 53.

78   Yves Chevaldonné, "'L'homme en morceaux, raccomodé': de Félicien Trevey au Professor Trewey," *1895* 36 (February 2002): 29–32, https://doi.org/10.4000/1895.132, http://journals.openedition.org/1895/132.

79   *Berliner Börsenzeitung*, August 9, 1881, 5.

80   Tom Gunning, "The Long and the Short of It: Centuries of Projecting Shadows, From Natural Magic to the Avant-Garde," in *Art of Projection*, ed. Stan Douglas and Christopher Eamon (Ostfildern: Hatje Cantz Verlag, 2009), 28.

81   "Hypnose im Film," *Neue Kino-Rundschau*, April 12, 1919, 7.

82   "Neuestes aus Deutschland," *Neue Kino-Rundschau*, October 2, 1920, 13.

83   "Filmnachrichten aus aller Welt," *Der Film-Bote*, April 26, 1924, 11.

84   Maria Tatar, *Spellbound: Studies on Mesmerism and Literature* (Princeton, NJ: Princeton University Press, 1978), 11.

85   Tatar, *Spellbound*, 14–15.

86   Tatar, *Spellbound*, 29.

87   Generally, Scottish physician James Braid is credited with having coined the term, first as "neuro-hypnotism," meaning nervous sleep, and then shortening this to "hypnotism"; he also used the term "neurypnology," shortened from "neuro-hypnology." Some sources, however, attribute the term to an earlier follower of Mesmer, Hénin de Cuvillers, who had suggested a number of different terms in the 1820s. See Tatar, *Spellbound*, 31; and Judith Pintar and Steven Jay Lynn, *Hypnosis: A Brief History* (Chichester: Wiley-Blackwell, 2008), 44.

88   Tatar, *Spellbound*, 31.

89   Heather Wolffram, "'An Object of Vulgar Curiosity': Legitimizing Medical Hypnosis in

Imperial Germany," *Journal of the History of Medicine and Allied Sciences* 67, no. 1 (January 2012): 151.

90 Paul Lerner, "Hysterical Cures: Hypnosis, Gender and Performance in World War I and Weimar Germany," *History Workshop Journal* 45 (Spring 1998): 81.

91 Lerner, "Hysterical Cures," 81.

92 For more details on Charcot's inherently theatrical production, see, for example: Rhona Justice-Malloy, "Charcot and the Theatre of Hysteria," *Journal of Popular Culture* 28, no. 4 (Spring 1995): 133–38.

93 Lerner, "Hysterical Cures," 82.

94 John Fletcher, *Freud and the Scene of Trauma* (New York: Fordham University Press, 2013), 11.

95 "Tagesneuheiten. [Wissenschaft und Hypnose]," *Linzer Tages-Post*, July 19, 1895, 3.

96 R. E., "Der Hypnotismus," *Salzburger Chronik für Stadt und Land*, November 8, 1893, 1, 3.

97 "Nachrichten aus Oberösterreich und Salzburg. Oberösterreichischer Volksbildungsverein," *Linzer Tages-Post*, February 20, 1895, 4.

98 Lerner, "Hysterical Cures," 82–83.

99 Lerner, "Hysterical Cures," 79–80.

100 Justinus, "Die Wachsuggestion in der Oeffentlichkeit. Gutachten des Berliner Polizeipräsidiums," *Neues Wiener Journal*, June 15, 1920, 4.

101 For an in-depth discussion of this, see Stefan Andriopoulos, *Possessed: Hypnotic Crimes, Corporate Fiction, and the Invention of Cinema* (Chicago, IL: University of Chicago Press, 2008).

102 See, for example: "Das hypnotische Verbrechen. Der Fall Marie D.," *Neues Wiener Journal*, May 10, 1921. See also "Hypnose vor Gericht," *Mittagblatt des Neuen Wiener Journals*, January 25, 1921.

103 Siegfried Kracauer, *From Caligari to Hitler: A Psychological History of the German Film* (Princeton, NJ: Princeton University Press, 2004), 112.

104 Kracauer, *From Caligari to Hitler*, 96.

105 Kracauer, *From Caligari to Hitler*, 113.

106 Kracauer's reference to the husband as "the count" fits with some versions of *Warning Shadows* that used alternate titles (or to the version released with added intertitles). For example, a French review of *Warning Shadows* from 1924 refers to the husband as "le comte de Schlosberg," the count of Schlosberg. Unsigned review of *Warning Shadows* (*Le Montreur d'Ombres*), *Cinemagazine*, September 5, 1924, 391.

107 Kracauer, *From Caligari to Hitler*, 114.

108 Kracauer, *From Caligari to Hitler*, 114.

109 I discuss the issues of power and gender that come into play in *Warning Shadows* in more depth in chapter 4 of my book, *Gender and the Uncanny in Films of the Weimar Republic* (Detroit, MI: Wayne State University Press, 2014).

110 Hugo Münsterberg, *Hugo Munsterberg on Film: The Photoplay; A Psychological Study and Other Writings*, ed. Allan Langdale (London: Routledge, 2001), 97.

111 Münsterberg, *Hugo Munsterberg on Film*, 98.

112 Münsterberg, *Hugo Munsterberg on Film*, 97.

113 Andreas Killen, "Weimar Cinema between Hypnosis and Enlightenment," in *Facing Fear: The History of an Emotion in Global Perspective*, ed. Michael Laffan and Max Weiss (Princeton, NJ: Princeton University Press, 2012), 95.

114 Killen, "Weimar Cinema between Hypnosis and Enlightenment," 101.

115 See, for example, Raymond Bellour's *Le Corps du cinema: hypnoses, émotions, animalités* [The Body of Cinema: Hypnoses, Emotions, Animalities] (Paris: POL/Trafic, 2009) or, for a discussion in English of that as yet untranslated book, see Hilary Radner and Alistair Fox, *Raymond Bellour: Cinema and the Moving Image* (Edinburgh: Edinburgh University Press, 2018).

116 Killen, "Weimar Cinema between Hypnosis and Enlightenment," 104.

117 Heide Schönemann, *Paul Wegener: Frühe Moderne im Film* (Stuttgart and London: Edition Axel Menges, 2003), 24.

118 Nancy Forgione, "'The Shadow Only': Shadow and Silhouette in Late Nineteenth-Century Paris," *The Art Bulletin* 81, no. 3 (September 1999): 493.

119 See, for example, the description in Georg Jacob, *Geschichte des Schattentheaters: Erweiterte Neubearbeitung des Vortrags; Das Schattentheater in seiner Wanderung vom Morgenland zum Abendland* (Berlin: Mayer & Müller, 1907), 127. Frances Guerin also notes the deviation of the silhouette play in *Warning Shadows* from the traditional form. Frances Guerin, *A Culture of Light: Cinema and Technology in 1920s Germany* (Minneapolis: University of Minnesota Press, 2005), 97–98.

120 Jacob, *Geschichte des Schattentheaters*, 156.

121 Schönemann, *Paul Wegener*, 24.

122 Schönemann, *Paul Wegener*, 27.

123 Rachel Palfreyman, "Life and Death in the Shadows: Lotte Reiniger's *Die Abenteuer des Prinzen Achmed*," *German Life and Letters* 64, no. 1 (January 2011): 8. See also Stephen Brockmann, "*Die Abenteuer des Prinzen Achmed* (1926): The Birth of the Feature-Length Animation Film," in his *Critical History of German Film*, 2nd edition (Rochester, NY: Camden House, 2020), 87–104.

124 T., "Der Avantgardefilm," *Mein Film* 175 (1929): 11.

125 Christian Metz, *Psychoanalysis and Cinema: The Imaginary Signifier*, trans. Celia Britton, Annwyl Williams, Ben Brewster, and Alfred Guzzetti (London: Macmillan, 1982), 45.

126 Jacob, *Geschichte des Schattentheaters*, 156.

127 Robison in Treuner, ed., *Filmkünstler: Wir über uns selbst*.

128 "Hypnose im Film," 7.

129 Christian Rogowski, "Preface," in *The Many Faces of Weimar Cinema: Rediscovering Germany's Filmic Legacy*, ed. Christian Rogowski (Rochester, NY: Camden House, 2010), xii.

130 Anton Kaes, "Silent Cinema," *Monatshefte* 82, no. 3 (Fall 1990): 247.

131 Karl Christian Führer, "Auf dem Weg zur 'Massenkultur'? Kino und Rundfunk in der Weimarer Republik," *Historische Zeitschrift* 262, no. 3 (June 1996): 742.

132 Richard Muckermann, "Einige Gedanken zur Psychologie des Kinos," *Süddeutsche Filmzeitung*, May 1, 1925, 4.

133 Kracauer, *From Caligari to Hitler*, 114.

134 "Demonstrationen in Berlin: Zusammenstöße zwischen Arbeitslosen und Polizei," *Vossische Zeitung*, October 16, 1923, 3.

135 "Dollar 4,1 Milliarden," *Vossische Zeitung*, October 16, 1923, 4.

136 Unsigned review of *Tragödie der Liebe*, *Der Kinematograph*, October 14, 1923, 5.

137 "Filmkritische Rundschau," *Der Kinematograph*, October 21, 1923, 6.

138 Walter Thielemann, "Berliner Brief," *Der Film-Bote*, November 10, 1923, 12.

139 Hildebrandt, "Schatten: Eine Analyse," 3.